Revised Edition

KNOWLEDGE WHIZZ 6

Kunal Savarkar Seema Chari

Collins

KNOWLEDGE WHIZZ 6

Revised Edition

Kunal Savarkar • Seema Chari

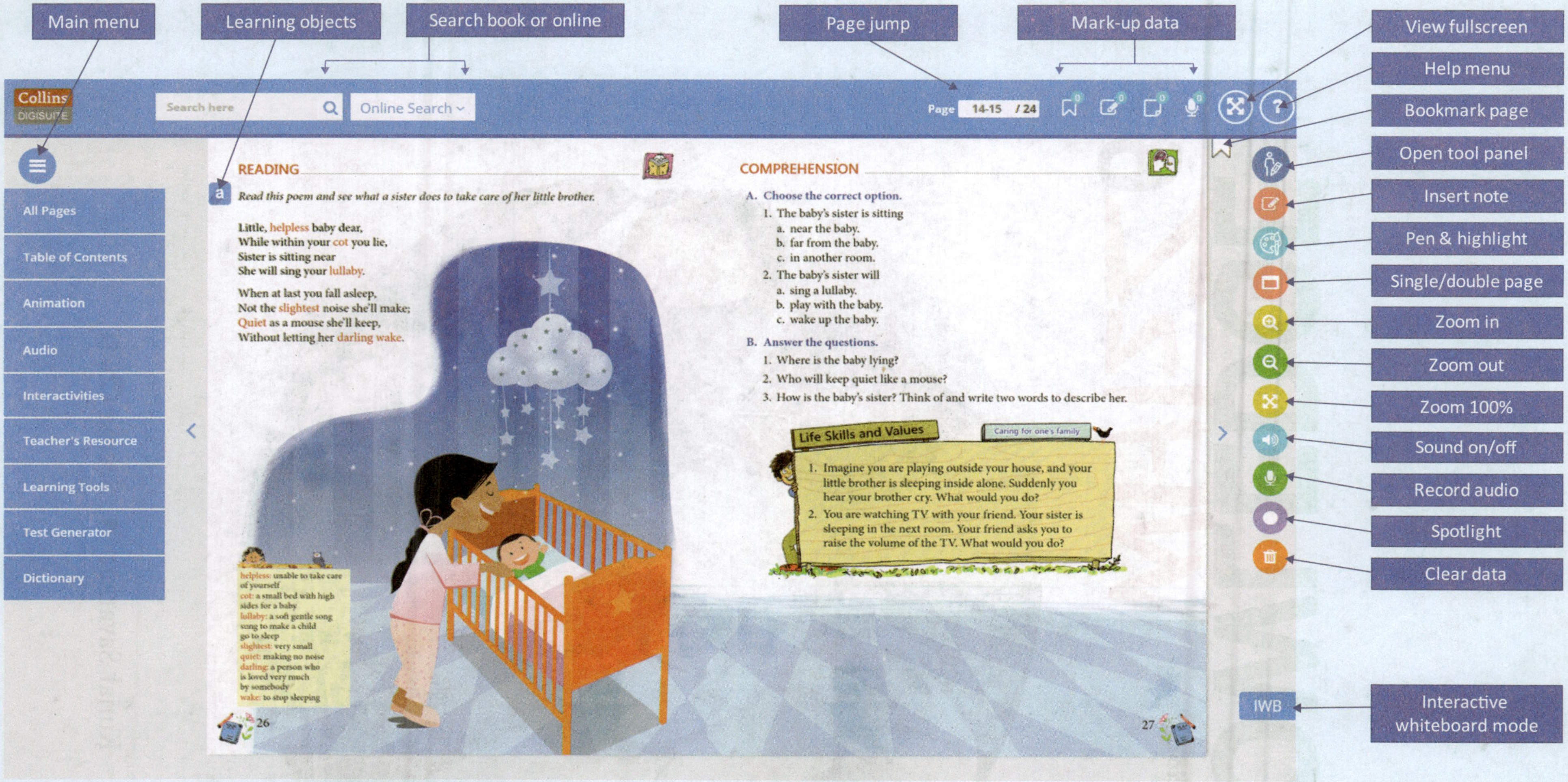

Student + Teacher

- **a** animations
- **ilt** instructor-led tutorials
- **ia** activities
- **w** worksheets
- audio
- **g** games
- **v** videos

Teacher-only

- **lp** lesson plans
- **w** worksheets
- **tn** teacher's notes
- **ak** answer keys

Preface

Welcome to ***Knowledge Whizz*** Version 2.0! Our belief that knowledge is for everyone has resonated well across the country, with thousands of school children now using the series, thereby reinforcing our conviction that general knowledge is not the exclusive preserve of a few quizzers. In this multimedia age, knowledge is everywhere, but sourcing, assimilating and recalling it is a skill that can be learned!

Knowledge Whizz, now in its second edition, is a unique series that aims to offer general knowledge covering a wide range of subjects, both curricular as well as extra-curricular, to children from six to thirteen years of age. These are GK books for learning, not quiz books for testing.

Salient features of the series

- Each task comprises at least two kinds of inputs to help children arrive at the answers and acquire knowledge at the same time.
- Tasks cover a wide range of topics presented with a twist. For instance, history includes the story of the automobile, bicycle, cinema, cricket and flight; science includes accidental inventions and discoveries; geography comes alive through associative information and culturally rich chapters. Language and literature cover trivia and etymology, two wonderful learning tools.
- Themes from modern life such as gaming, media, business and finance are extensively explored as well as tidbits about the quirky and the quotidian.
- India-specific content presented beautifully through fun, richly illustrated tasks, designed to whet the curiosity of children and inspire them to explore their beautiful country in all its diversity. New chapters on North East India bring the vibrancy and uniqueness of this relatively lesser known part of India to children everywhere.
- The books do not expect children to be pre-equipped with knowledge but instead reward inquisitiveness by giving them workoutable tasks.
- The artistic and colourful layouts make the presentation more accessible, exciting and alluring whilst facilitating self-learning.
- Special features are an exciting mixed bag of environment education, life skills, values, quick quizzes, cool facts, cool activity, evaluation of multiple intelligences and Higher Order Thinking Skills to make children become well-rounded individuals.
- Brand new features incorporated into Version 2.0 include Aptitudes, aiming to hone and cement specific verbal, visual and logical aptitudes through the common lens of general knowledge, Safety Science, which draws our attention tn the science behind the measures we should take to stay safe wherever we are, and Game, to bring a good dose of fun into learning.

We gratefully acknowledge the contribution of the Xpress Minds Edutainment team, whose inputs have been invaluable for this second edition.

We are certain that this series will open up the world of general knowledge and make learning a fun, instinctive and rewarding process for all.

~ Kunal Savarkar and Seema Chari

In This Book ...

Dances of the World

A. *Find the names of eighteen popular dance forms from around the world in this word search.*

A	H	I	P	H	O	P	B	T	Y	B	E	L	L	F	A
C	O	E	J	L	S	C	P	K	O	Q	S	U	A	G	J
D	P	F	I	P	A	J	O	Z	C	B	S	A	M	B	A

Multiple Intelligence tasks focus on the 8 Intelligences: interpersonal, intrapersonal, bodily kinesthetic, visual-spatial, logical reasoning, verbal-linguistic, naturalistic and musical. Each page explores 5-6 intelligences to encourage learners to learn in their own way and is not to be used for assessment.

Higher Order Thinking Skills (HOTS) pages encourage critical thinking and teach learners to analyse and evaluate information. Cool quizmaster, Kunal Savarkar, helps students become knowledge detectives and skilled quizzers.

Stamp Collecting

Stamps are a great way to learn about the history and culture of its people. The world's first postage stamp was issued in the United Kingdom in 1840 and is called the 'Penny Black'. In 1852, the 'Scinde Dawk' became the first stamp to be issued in India.

Cool Activity
Fun activities to learn through doing.

Cool Quiz
Encourages research to find solutions.

Current Affairs
Visit **www.collins.in/knowledgewhizz** for Current Affairs updates and weekly quizzes.

Snakes and Ladders

When you are walking on the pavement/ crossing the road by foot, you are called a pedestrian. Play this game of snakes and ladders and see how

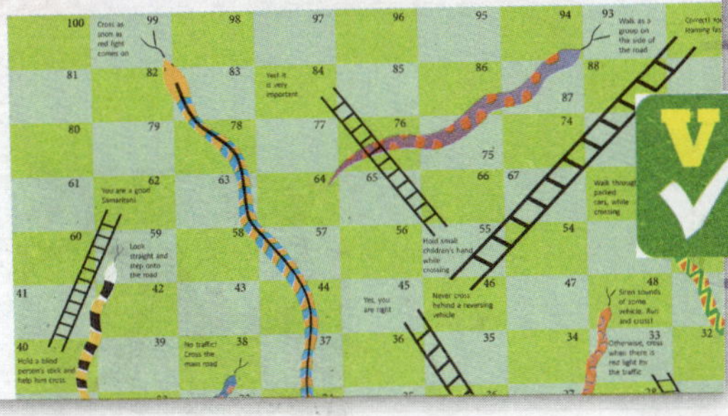

Values pages focus on inculcating values, morals, ethics and right attitudes in students through to-do tasks.

Aptitude

Aptitude Tasks are designed to teach children to develop specific skills such as sequencing, classification, analogies and others through rebuses, matching, sorting and pattern activities, with step-by-step tips on how to solve them.

Life Skills pages expose learners to problems in real-life situations to help them learn to take decisions.

At the Post Office

The world is moving away from real hard letters to email and other means of electro communication. But in India, the post offi importance as it connects every nook and vast country. So 'snail mail' is still an ever

COOL FACT

The inner margins of the leaves of a bound book are called gutters. The printed or unprinted paper cover, placed around the bound book is called a jacket.

Green Earth

Green Earth page focuses on environmental issues and imbibes the right attitude towards conservation of environment.

COOL FACT

Factoids linked to the content of the page. The fun element in them will make you say, 'Hey! Cool to know that.'

Safety Science

Safety is not just a notion; it is a science, which means it is guided by research, facts and figures. From home to school, public places to controlled environments, we can do a lot to keep ourselves safe. The Safety Science chapters in each book show us how.

Game

Life is a game! Each book in the series has at least one puzzle, maze or strategy-based activity, always with a GK twist, but with the added feel-good incentive of "winning the game".

Quiz Yourself are quick quizzes to assess what the children have learned in the book. The main themes and the cool facts will all form the basis of the Quiz Yourself section, intended as a self-evaluation tool from books 3 to 8.

Detailed Contents

Contents

All About Books

Use the clues to write down answers in the word grid. Then read the shaded letters from top to bottom to get the final answer.

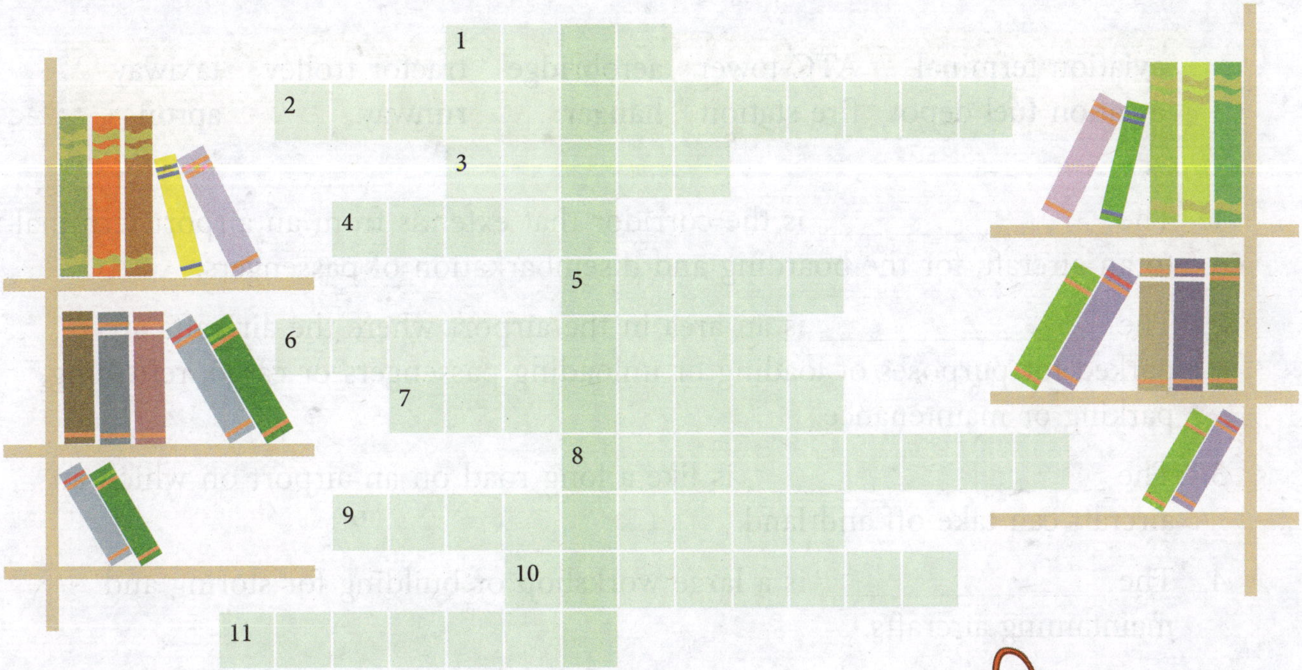

1. Acronym of International Standard Book Number
2. Story written by a person about his own life
3. A story, usually about animals, that has a moral at the end
4. A non-real story whose length spans an entire book
5. An alphabetical list of names, topics etc., which tells you on which page of the book they are mentioned
6. An alternative name used by a writer instead of his real name
7. Parts into which a book is divided
8. Book bound in a protective stiff cover jacket like cardboard or leather
9. A person or company that releases the book in the market
10. List at the end of the book giving special words and their meanings
11. An introduction to the book mentioning what is written and why

Now check if the middle column matches this description.
One who loves books is called a ________________.

COOL FACT

The inner margins of the leaves of a bound book are called gutters. The printed or unprinted paper cover, placed around the bound book is called a jacket.

At the Airport

A. *An airport is a buzzing hive of activity. Fill in the blanks about special areas in the airport with words from the list of options.*

aviation terminal	ATC tower	aerobridge	tractor trolley	taxiway
aviation fuel depot	fire station	hangar	runway	apron

1. The ________________ is the corridor that extends from an airport terminal to an aircraft, for the boarding and disembarkation of passengers.
2. The ________________ is an area in the airport where the aircrafts are parked for purposes of loading or unloading passengers or cargo, refuelling, parking or maintenance.
3. The ____________________ is like a long road on an airport on which an aircraft can take off and land.
4. The ________________ is a large workshop or building for storing and maintaining aircrafts.
5. The air traffic controllers of the ________________ coordinate the movement of thousands of aircraft to keep them at safe distances from each other. They also direct them during take off and landing from airports, around bad weather and ensure that traffic flows smoothly with minimal delays.
6. The building in the airport where the arrival and departure of the passengers is handled is called the ________________.
7. The ______________________ in the airport is where a specialized type of petroleum-based fuel, used to power aircraft is stored in tanks.
8. Airports have a ________________ to handle accidents caused due to fire.
9. A ________________ is a path on an airport connecting runways with ramps, hangars, terminals and other facilities.
10. A ________________ carries luggage from the aircraft to the baggage vestibules, where passengers can collect their luggage.

B. *Now put the correct number in the circles next to that area in the picture.*

COOL FACT India's first airport was Mumbai's Juhu Aerodrome, established in 1928. Today, India's biggest and busiest airport is the Indira Gandhi International Airport, Delhi, with traffic of almost 58 million passengers in 2016-17.

3

Bird Facts

Use the clues given below to write the names of twelve interesting birds.

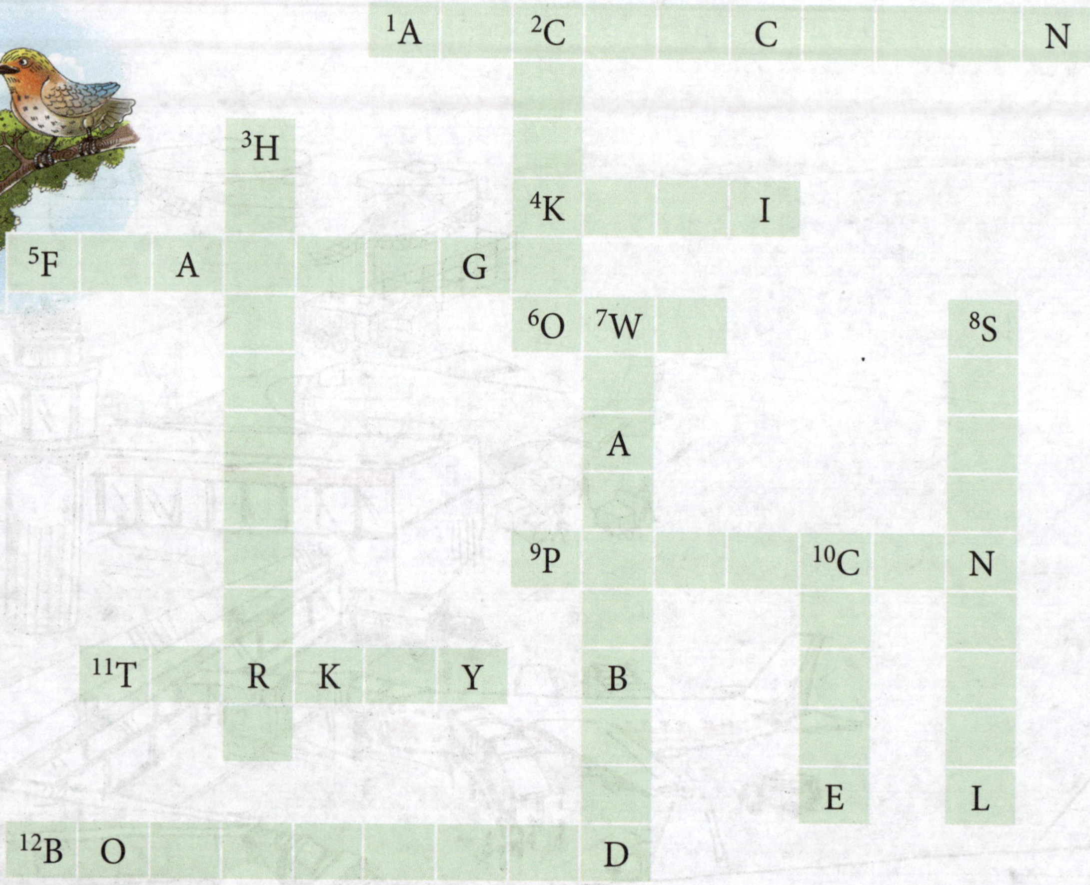

1.

This bird makes the longest annual migratory journey.

2.

This bird tricks other birds into hatching her eggs and raising her offspring.

3.

This bird collects nectar by hovering in the air, in front of flowers.

4. This flightless bird is a native of New Zealand.

5. This tall, wading bird has pink or red feathers.

6. This hunter uses its acute sense of hearing to locate prey in the night.

7. The male of this species makes a nest to attract females.

8. The name of this large, wading bird is derived from the shape of its unique beak that looks like a spoon.

9. A large waterbird with a long beak and a large, bag-like pouch around the throat.

10. One of the largest flying birds, it is called *Saras* in India.

11. This North American bird shares its name with a country too.

12. This bird, a native of Australia and New Guinea, can also mimic mobile phone ringtones.

COOL FACT

Auk birds live in the northern hemisphere. Similar to penguins of the southern hemisphere with their black and white coats, auks can also fly.

INDIA

4 Great Women of India

A. *Using the pictures and descriptions as clues, identify these great women of India.*

Picture	Description
1. 	Born as Mehrunissa, she married the Mughal Emperor Jahangir in 1611 and became the Empress of India. ________________________
2. 	The Queen of Kittur who lead an armed rebellion against the British, but was defeated in 1824. ________________________
3. 	Emperor Asoka's daughter, she became a Buddhist nun and is credited with the establishment of the Bhikkhuni Sangha. ________________________
4. 	The Rani of Jhansi who fought bravely against the British in the 1857 War of Independence. ________________________

5. 

Called the Rajmata, she was the mother of Chhatrapati Shivaji Maharaj, who was crowned king in 1674.

____

6. 

The valiant and pious Maratha queen who ruled central India from 1767 onwards from her capital at Maheshwar.

____

7. 

She became the first woman ruler of the Delhi Sultanate in 1236.

____

Ahilyabai Holkar	Sanghamitra	Nur Jahan	Jijabai
Rani Chennamma	Rani Lakshmibai	Razia Sultan	

B. *Now arrange these women in chronological order. Use the descriptive clues to help place them. One has been done for you.*

300 BCE	1205 -1240 CE	1577-1645 CE	1598 -1674 CE	1725 -1795 CE	1778 -1829 CE	1828 -1858 CE
Sanghamitra						

COOL FACT The Taj Mahal at Agra was built by Emperor Shah Jahan as the final resting place for his wife, Mumtaz Mahal, who was the niece of Nur Jahan.

The Number 6

Six is the smallest positive whole number which is neither a square number nor a prime number. But apart from its mathematical uniqueness, there are many interesting facts that are all connected with the number six.

A. *Here are six unique facts about the number six!*

1. The basic grid of the ________ alphabet for the blind comprises of six dots. Sixty four different signs can be created from those six dots.
2. All ________ have six legs.
3. The singular of ________ is die. Each die has six sides.
4. The number of tastes in traditional Indian medicine ________ is six. They are—sweet, sour, salty, bitter, pungent, and astringent. These tastes are used to suggest a diet based on the symptoms of the body.
5. ________ are six babies born at the same time to their mother.
6. Some people have a sixth finger on one or both hands. This condition is called ________.

dice
Sextuplets
insects
Braille
Ayurveda
hexadactyly

B. *Now answer these six questions all of which have something to do with the number 6. The answers are in the help box. But beware, there are six incorrect options too.*

1. Which country in Europe is also called the Hexagon due to its shape?
2. Six-pack is a term that is usually used to describe a set of well-developed muscles in which part of the body?
3. Which cricket playing island nation has six states?
4. What is the airline code of Indigo, one of India's largest airlines?
5. Which House of the Indian Parliament has members elected for six-year terms?
6. Which was the sixth book in the Harry Potter series?

COOL FACT

'The sixth sick sheik's sixth sheep's sick' is one of the toughest tongue twisters in the English language. Try saying it quickly!

Lok Sabha	Sri Lanka	Spain	6E	Rajya Sabha
Australia	6W	France	Abdomen	Arm
Harry Potter and the Order of the Phoenix			Harry Potter and the Half-Blood Prince	

5

Capital Cities and Rivers

The great rivers of the Earth have been the starting point of some of the greatest cities.

Match these country capitals with the rivers on which they have been founded. To help you, we have given you the rough geographical location of the rivers within brackets. One has been done for you.

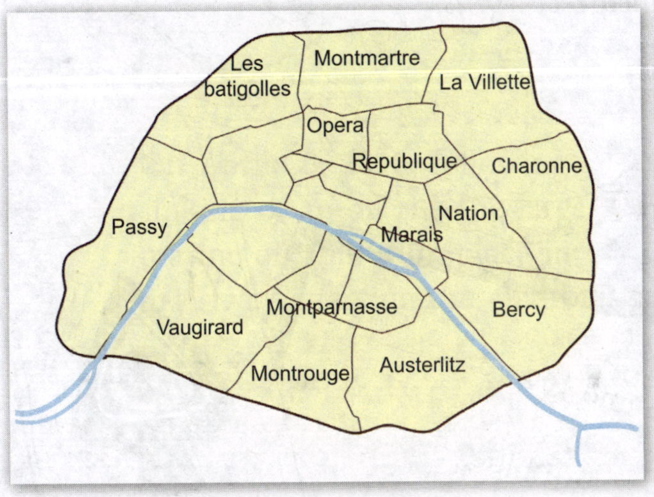

Paris and the Seine*

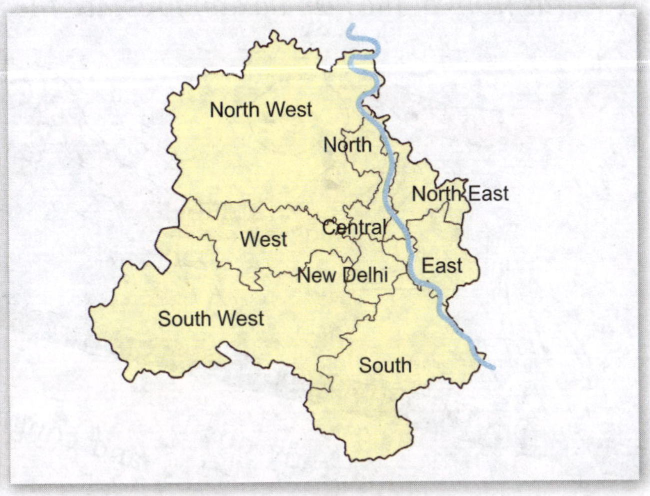

Delhi and the Yamuna*

1.	Rome	a.	Yamuna (South Asia)
2.	Paris	b.	Tigris (Middle East)
3.	London	c.	Bagmati (South Asia)
4.	Cairo	d.	Rio de la Plata (South America)
5.	Washington, DC	e.	Seine (Continental Europe)
6.	Delhi	f.	Thames (Western Europe)
7.	Moscow	g.	Tiber (Southern Europe)
8.	Baghdad	h.	Moskva (Eastern Europe)
9.	Kathmandu	i.	Nile (North Africa)
10.	Buenos Aires	j.	Potomac (North America)

*Artistic rendition

COOL FACT The Danube is the river that flows by the maximum number of national capitals in the world—Bratislava, Belgrade, Vienna and Budapest. Do you know the countries whose capital cities these are?

Pronunciation

English is a beautiful language, but it has more exceptions than rules when it comes to pronunciation.

Read this fragment of a poem. Some words are underlined. They do not belong in the poem, but they rhyme with the correct words in the help box. Pick correct words from of the help box and replace the incorrect words.

... I take it you already no 1. ______
Of tough and cow 2. ______ and cough and toe 3. ______?
Others may stumble, but not you,
On hiccough, thorough, stuff 4. ______, and blue 5. ______?

Well done! And now you wish, perhaps
To learn of less familiar traps?
Beware of heard, a dreadful word,
That looks like weird 6. ______ and sounds like curd 7. ______.

And dead; it's said like led 8. ______, not seed 9. ______;
For goodness sake, don't call it deed!
Watch out for meat and great and threat;
They rhyme with neat 10. ______ and
wait 11. ______ and wet 12. ______.

A moth is not a moth in mother,
Nor loath 13. ______ in bother, broth in brother.
And here is not a match for where 14. ______,
Or dear and clear 15. ______ for bear and pear.

And then there's dose and <u>hose</u> ______ and <u>whose</u> ______,
Just look them up, and goose 16. choose. 17.
And <u>stork</u> ______ and <u>shirk</u> ______ and <u>hard</u>
18. and ward, 19. ______ and word and
20. ______ font and <u>hunt</u> ______. 21.
<u>board</u> ______ 22.
And do and go, then <u>wart</u> ______ and 23.
<u>heart</u> ______.
Come 24. come, I've hardly made a start.
A dreadful language? Why, man alive,
I'd learned to talk it when I was five.

And yet to write it, the more I tried,
I hadn't learned it at fifty-five!

know	bough
dough	slough
through	beard
bird	bead
suite	straight
debt	both
there	fear
lose	cork
work	card
front	sword
thwart	cart
bed	rose

COOL FACT The words month, orange, purple and silver have no rhyming words in the English language.

7

Footprints of Birds and Animals

In the columns below, the first column has feet of animals or birds, the second has the silhouettes of their footprints and the third column has the names. Match the feet, the footprints and the names by drawing connecting lines.

1. 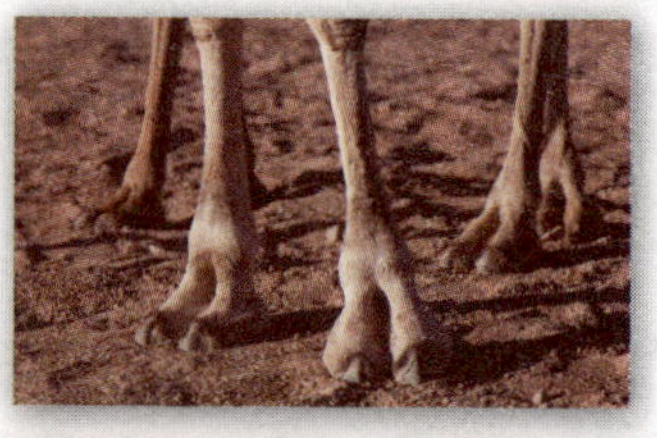
2. 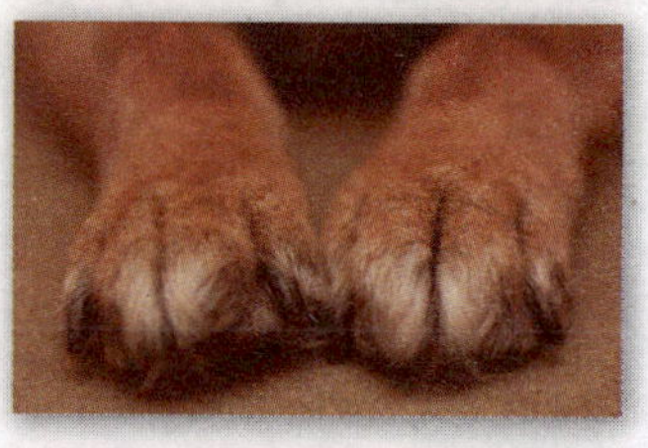
3. 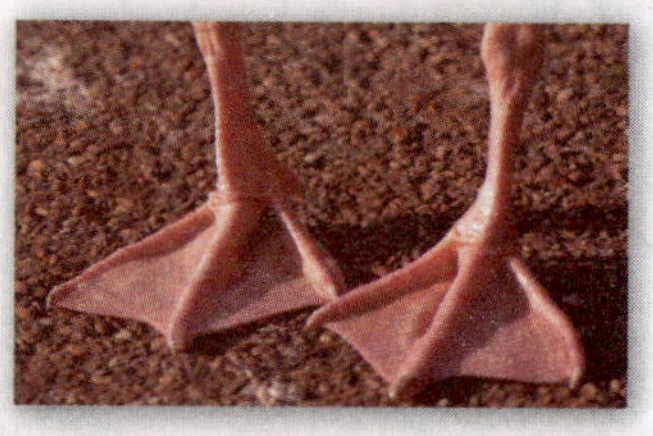
4. 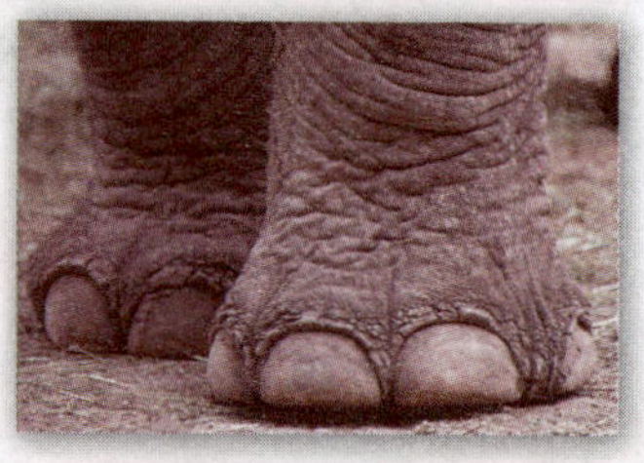
5. 
6. 

a. 

b. 

c. 

d. 

e. 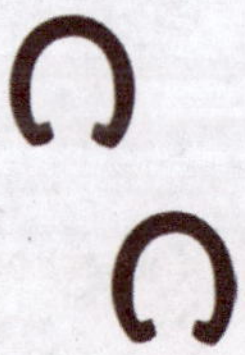

f. 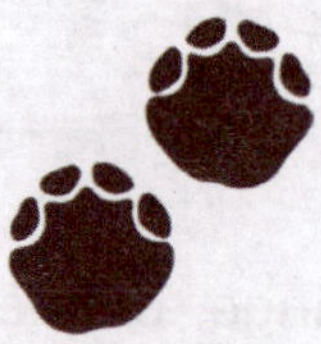

i. Dog

ii. Elephant

iii. Duck

iv. Camel

v. Horse

vi. Giraffe

7. 	g. 	vii. Bear
8. 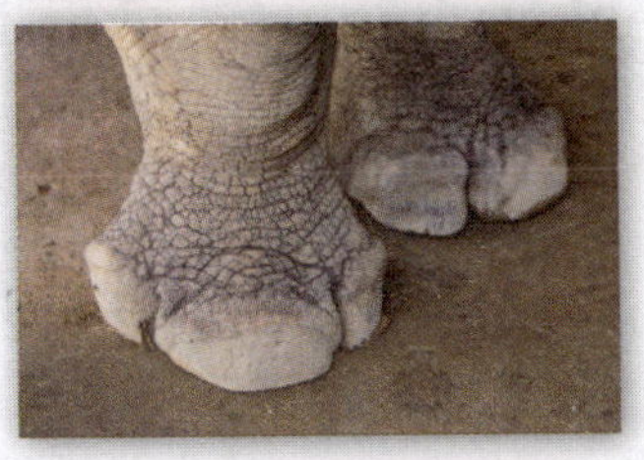	h. 	viii. Ostrich
9. 	i. 	ix. Tortoise
10. 	j. 	x. Kangaroo
11. 	k. 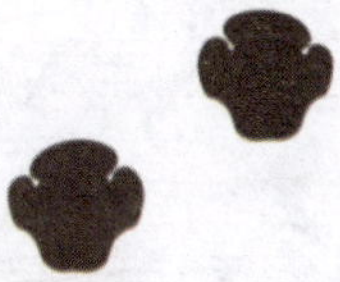	xi. Lion
12. 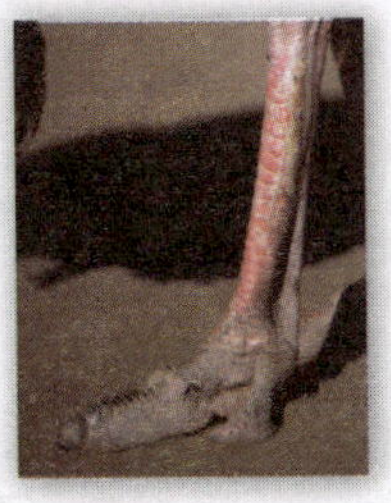	l. 	xii. Rhinoceros

COOL FACT

Pugmark is the term used to refer to the footprint of most animals. They are unique to each species as well as individual members within the species. Identifying and tracking pugmarks can help in estimating the populations of wild animals.

At the Post Office

The world is moving away from hard copy letters to emails and other means of electronic communication. But in India, the post office still enjoys importance as it connects every nook and corner of this vast country. So snail mail is still an everyday reality here.

A. *Have you ever thought about the journey of a letter? Rearrange the steps and trace its journey in the correct order.*

a. 

The letter is collected by the postman and sorted at the post office.

b. 

Write a letter on a sheet of paper, fold and place in an envelope.

c. 

The letter is sent by road/rail/ aeroplane/ship to the destination.

d. 

Post your letter in a letter box.

e. 

It is again sorted on the basis of the destination address.

COOL FACT The distance between cities is always measured as the distance between their general post offices. This is done for all Indian cities, except Delhi, where the distance is calculated from Raj Ghat.

f.

A date seal is affixed on the stamp to show when the letter is sorted at the sender's post office

g.

A stamp is affixed according to the weight.

h.

The local postman hands the letter over at the recipient's house.

B. *The post office is not just a place where letters and parcels are sorted. Complete these statements with services offered by the postal department. Choose the answers from the help box.*

1. The quickest way of sending a letter by post from one city to another is by using ________________.
2. Money can be transferred between two people living in different parts of the country using the ________________ facility.
3. You can find the value of stamps to be affixed on a parcel post by getting it weighed and evaluated at the ________________.
4. You will not find ________________ in an Indian Post Office.
5. The ________________ already has a stamp printed on it, so you do not need to affix extra stamps.
6. A collector of postal stamps is known as a ________________.
7. The day a new stamp is released, a ________________ is issued.
8. ________________ is also a service provided by the post office.

money order	speed post	post office counter
first day cover	philatelist	house rent collection
inland letter	passport form collection	

8

Adventure Sports

Adventure sports require both skill and courage. Here is an open crossword based on adventure sports. Solve the crossword using the clues.

Across

4. A sport in which a person enters a large transparent ball which is then rolled along the ground or downhill.
5. The short form of Bicycle Motocross—a sport where contestants use bicycles to race across specially designed or natural tracks.
6. An activity in which participants climb up or down natural rocks or artificial rock faces.
8. A sport that requires snowy slopes and has two main types named—Nordic and Alpine.
9. A sport in which persons 'ride' the waves that break onto the seashore.
10. An adventure on foot—a combination of hiking and walking especially in mountainous areas.

Down

1. An exciting activity in which natural cave systems are explored.
2. A sport, in which a person jumps from an aircraft or high point like a cliff wearing a wide, rectangular, steerable parachute.
3. A type of motorcycle racing performed on rough terrain.
5. An activity where a person leaps from a height, usually head first, but is secured by a long, strong nylon-cased cord around the ankles.
7. An exciting activity involving moving down a fast-flowing river, especially over rapids, in an inflatable boat.

Cool Activity

Power blocking, slacklining and limbo skating are examples of extreme sports. Find out what they mean, but DO NOT attempt them. There is a reason they are called extreme sports. They should not be attempted without proper training and supervision.

COOL FACT

David Belle is considered to be the founder of Parkour, an adventure sport in which a participant aims to get from point A to point B in the most efficient way possible.

INDIA

9

Indian Music Decoded

Solve this crossword based on terms from Indian music using the clues given below.

COOL FACT

All ragas composed by the legendary singer, Mian Tansen, are prefixed with the words *Mian ki/ka* as a tribute to him. Well-known of these are *Mian ki Todi* and *Mian ka Sarang*.

Clues

Across

2. A disciple who undertakes to learn from a guru
4. Tamil word for a concert or a musical event
5. A type of composition in Carnatic music
8. A form of music associated with Sufi mystics
9. School or style of singing, like Gwalior, Delhi or Agra
10. A form of Urdu poetry that is often sung

Down

1. In Indian music, the smallest interval of pitch that the human ear can hear
3. A form of devotional poetry from Maharashtra
6. A style of light classical singing
7. An Urdu word which means tune or music

World Famous Statues

Here are some of the world's most famous statues. In many cases, the statue is the best known landmark of the city itself. Match the images with the cities where they are found.

1. 
The Motherland Calls

2. 
Statue of Liberty

3. 
Christ the Redeemer

4. 
Merlion

5. 
Statue of David

6. 
Statue of Four Rivers

7. 
Little Mermaid

8. 
Rodin's 'The Thinker'

9. 
Eros

10. 
Mannekin Pis

a. New York, USA
b. Rio de Janeiro, Brazil
c. Volgograd, Russia
d. Florence, Italy
e. Copenhagen, Denmark
f. Paris, France
g. Rome, Italy
h. Singapore
i. Piccadilly Circus, London, UK
j. Brussels, Belgium

COOL FACT One of the oldest statues in the world is the 4,500 year old small bronze figure of the Dancing Girl which was found at Mohenjo Daro.

Let's Visit Nepal

Capital: Kathmandu

Currency: Nepalese Rupee

Official Language: Nepali

The beautiful Himalayan country of Nepal lies between India and China.

Fill in these blanks about Nepal with the words given in the help box.

earthquake	Lalitpur	Patan	Bhaktapur	yeti	Karnali
Gurkhas	*khukri*	Sagarmatha	Kanchenjunga	Sikkim	

1. Kathmandu, the capital of this ancient country, includes three older cities—______________, ______________ and ______________.
2. In a popular legend, there are tales of an Abominable Snowman that roams the snowy slopes and scares mountaineers and trekkers-*Him Manav*. In the local language, it is known as the ___________.
3. Nepal is home to the brave ________________, some of whom also serve in the Indian Army. These warriors are known for carrying a traditional knife called a ______________.
4. Nepal is home to eight of the world's ten tallest mountains including Mt Everest, locally called ______________. The world's third tallest peak ______________________________ is situated on its border with the Indian state of ______________.
5. The longest river in Nepal is the ___________________.
6. On April 25th, 2015, Nepal was hit by an __________________ of magnitude 7.8 on the richter scale, the worst to hit the country in eighty years.

COOL FACT

The Nepalese flag is the world's only flag to have an irregular shape—two triangles. It has a red background, the same colour as the country's national flower, the rhododendron, with the sun and moon in it signifying that Nepal will exist as long as the sun and moon exist.

Time Zones

At any given moment, it is a different time at a different place in the world as indicated in the map. Time is calculated based on the Greenwich Mean Time or GMT.

COOL FACT

Russia is a very large country with eleven time zones. This means that when it is 10:00 pm at one end of the country, it is already 8 am of the next day at the other end.

Indian Standard Time (IST) is five hours and thirty minutes ahead of the GMT.

At 5:30 p.m. in India, what would the time be in these cities? Mark the time on the clock faces by drawing the hands.

1. 

Tokyo
(+3.30 hours)

2. 

San Francisco
(-13.30 hours)

3. 

Washington
(-10.30 hours)

4. 

London
(-5.30 hours)

5. 

Colombo
(same time)

6. 

Rome
(-4.30 hours)

7. 

Sydney
(+5.30 hours)

8. 

Dubai
(-1.30 hours)

9. 

Islamabad
(-0.30 hours)

10. 

Moscow
(-2.30 hours)

11. 

Cape Town
(-3.30 hours)

12. 

Rio de Janeiro
(-7.30 hours)

Faiths of the World

India is a secular country and people follow many different faiths.

Complete these statements about some of India's major religions. Each statement has two blanks. The answers are in the help box.

1. The Old Testament or ____________ is the sacred book of Judaism. Followers of this religion are known as ________.
2. The will of *Allah* is made known through the sacred text called the ______________, which he revealed to his messenger ______________.
3. ______________ ______________, one of the sacred texts of Hinduism, is essentially a dialogue that happened between the Pandava Prince _________ and his charioteer and guide, Krishna, during the Mahabharata war at Kurukshetra.
4. ____________ originated in the 1st century CE based on the life and teachings of ___________, who was born at Bethlehem.
5. _______________________, founded in the 15th century, is based on the teachings of its ten gurus. The first guru was Guru Nanak, who founded this faith. Their religious text is called the ________________________________.

6. Zoroastrianism is an ancient religion, founded by Zarathustra in Iran. The ________________ is the primary collection of sacred texts of this religion. In India, the followers of this religion are commonly known as ________________.

7. ________________________________ founded Buddhism sometime in the 6th century BCE. The sacred texts of Buddhism are collectively known as ________________, which literally means 'three baskets'.

8. ____________ is an Indian religion whose sacred texts are collectively known as the Agamas. The texts are based on the teachings of the religion's 24th and last Tirthankara, ________________.

Mahavira	Bhagavad Gita
Tanakh	Arjuna
Quran	Christianity
Sikhism	Prophet Mohammad PBUH
Jesus Christ	Zend Avesta
Parsis	Jainism
Tipitaka	Guru Granth Sahib
Jews	Gautama Buddha

COOL FACT

The Bahá'í Faith was founded by Bahá'u'lláh in the 19th century CE and is known for its beautiful temples worldwide, including the Lotus Temple at New Delhi.

LANGUAGE AND LITERATURE

11 Kangaroo and Joey Words

Kangaroo words are long words that contain smaller words having almost the same meaning. Such words are called Joeys. The letters in the joey appear in the same order as in the kangaroo word. For example, PRECIPITATION—RAIN.

Find the joey words from this list of fourteen kangaroo words and fill the grid. One has been done for you.

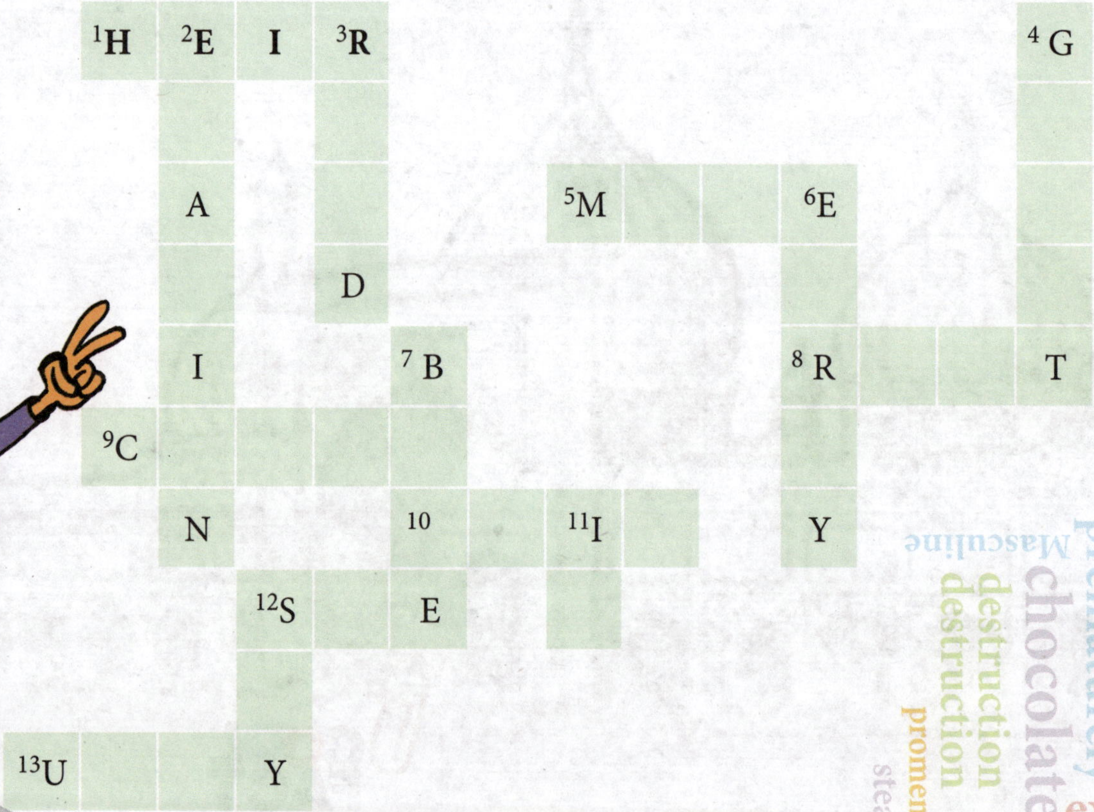

observe
unsightly
respite
prematurely
chocolate
exhilaratio
Masculine
destruction
destruction
promenade
stealthy

1. After her grandmother's demise, she became the **inheritor** of all her jewellery.

2. The show was such a huge success that all the performers felt a great feeling of **exhilaration**.

3. The park had a lovely leafy **promenade** running through it where people could walk, jog or skate.

4. There is a **gigantic** bouncing castle in the middle of the mall, where small children can jump and play.

5. Till as recently as fifty years ago, fashion designing, nursing and flight attendants were not considered **masculine** professions, but today, many men practise them without any biases.

6. The baby was born **prematurely**, much sooner than expected.

7. The top of the hill was a **barren** stretch of land, with not a tree or shrub in sight.

8. With temperatures crossing forty degrees all week, we got no **respite** from the heat.

9. The **chocolate** bean is one of Brazil's most famous exports.

10. The earthquake left a trail of **destruction** in its wake.

11. The earthworm **exists** inside the mud. It comes out when it rains.

12. Take a look through the microscope. What do you **observe**?

12. The fox moved through the forest in a quiet and **stealthy** manner.

13. After his accident, his leg was covered in **unsightly** scars for a month.

COOL FACT There can be many joeys inside a single kangaroo word. For example *fed*, *ate* and *eat* can all be found in the word *feasted*.

12

India and the Nobel Prize

The Nobel Prize is one of the highest decorations possible. Several Indians have received this award, including some who were born in India but lived and worked in other countries, later.

Match the face and description with these Nobel Prize Winners from India.

1. 

2. 

3. 

4. 

a. Rabindranath Tagore

b. CV Raman

c. Mother Teresa

d. Amartya Sen

i. First Asian to win a Nobel Prize

ii. Born in Albania, founder of Missionaries of Charity

iii. Child genius who won a Nobel Prize for Physics

iv. Economics prize winner

v. Founder of Bachpan Bachao Andolan

vi. Astrophysicist and nephew of CV Raman

vii. Received the Nobel Prize for Medicine

viii. Received the Nobel Prize for his work on the ribosome

e. Har Gobind Khorana

f. Kailash Satyarthi

g. Venkatraman Ramakrishnan

h. Subrahmanyan Chandrasekhar

5. 

6. 

7. 

8. 

COOL FACT

Ronald Ross (Medicine, 1902) and Rudyard Kipling (Literature, 1907) are both Englishmen who were born in India and who have received the Nobel Prize.

SCIENCE

13

Face Science

Read these statements about some of the strange things that happen to our eyes, ears, nose and throat. Write True for the true statements and False for the false ones. Also, correct the four false statements by writing the letter of one of the corrected statements provided below.

1. A newborn baby cries but sheds no tears as its tear glands develop later. ______________
2. Blinking washes the eyes with tears and helps keep the eyeball from getting dry. ______________
3. We yawn only when we feel sleepy. ______________
4. When you suck air into your throat suddenly, it hits the voice box, your vocal cords close suddenly and you get hiccups. ______________
5. If you yawn or swallow something, your ears will get blocked. ______________
6. Cold food or drinks can cause sneezing. ______________
7. Snoring is caused by the narrowing of the air passages in the nose, mouth and throat. ______________
8. If you drink too much water, you will get a runny nose. ______________

Corrected statements

a. If you yawn or swallow something, blocked ears will pop.

b. You get a runny nose because of the increased production of water by the mucous membrane.

c. We yawn even if we see someone else yawn.

d. Sneezing is caused due to the irritants that enter our noses and sinuses.

COOL FACT The human ear and nose bridge are made up of a substance softer than bone but less flexible than muscle called cartilage. Surprisingly, another animal whose entire skeleton is made up of cartilage is the shark.

Let's Go West

How much do you know about the states of Maharashtra, Gujarat, Rajasthan and Goa?

Read these statements about the states of western India and write MH for Maharashtra, GJ for Gujarat, RJ for Rajasthan or GA for Goa in the spaces given.

1. This state and Gujarat were once part of the Bombay Presidency.
2. This state shares land borders with Gujarat, Madhya Pradesh, Uttar Pradesh, Haryana and Punjab.
3. The Portuguese ruled this state until 1961.
4. The Rann of Kutch is situated in this state.
5. The historic cities of Bikaner, Jaisalmer and Udaipur are in this state.
6. The capital of this state is named after a freedom fighter.
7. You can find the forts of Sinhagad, Raigad and Daulatabad in this state.
8. This state is known for its beautiful beaches including Anjuna, Calangute and Varca.
9. Cricket superstar Sachin Tendulkar was born in this state.
10. This state has the longest coastline in India because of two large gulfs that jut into it.
11. India conducted nuclear tests in 1974 and 1998 at Pokhran, situated in this state.
12. This is the smallest state in India.

COOL FACT

The state of Rajasthan is India's largest state with a land area of 342,239 square kilometres. It was known as Rajputana prior to Independence. The Rajputs, a martial community, ruled over this area for centuries.

14

Sports and Numbers

All answers to the questions in Column A are numbers. In case you do not know the answers, read the clues in Column B. The answers are exactly the same.

Column A	Column B	Number
1. What is the maximum number of umpires found on court in a professional tennis match?	The number of Sachin Tendulkar's and Lionel Messi's jerseys	
2. How many players can represent one team on the court in a game of basketball?	The number of interlocking rings in the Olympic flag	
3. How many runners are there in an athletics relay team?	The number of suits in a deck of cards	
4. What is the value of the first point of a game in a lawn tennis match?	Product of the first three odd numbers	
5. What is the approximate distance of a marathon event in kilometres?	The sum of all the numbers on a pair of dice	
6. How many holes are there in a standard round of golf?	Age at which you can legally get a driving licence to drive a car in India	
7. How many trial attempts are allowed in a long jump event?	Number of primary colours	
8. How many pieces are there on a chessboard at the beginning of a game?	A full set of teeth in an adult human	

COOL FACT

Not all golf balls have the same number of dimples. Golf balls have from 330 to 500 dimples depending on the company which designs the ball. The ideal ball will usually have between 380 and 432 dimples.

LANGUAGE AND LITERATURE

15

Pen Names

Authors sometimes adopt a different name, called a pen name, to hide their real identities.

Read the clues about some of them and complete this crossword with their famous pen names. Some letters have been given to help you.

COOL FACT Some authors have chosen pen names that are less known than their real ones. Among them was India's nobel laureate, Rabindranath Tagore, who adopted the name Bhanu Singha, JK Rowling, the creator of the Harry Potter series, who also writes for older readers under the pen name, Robert Galbraith, and Enid Blyton, who briefly wrote under the name Mary Pollock

Across:

1. Samuel Langhorne Clemens, 19th century American humourist, author, and lecturer, creator of the immortal characters Tom Sawyer and Huckleberry Finn (4, 5)

4. Sampooran Singh Kalra, noted Indian poet, lyricist, director, and playwright, who works primarily in Hindi and Urdu (6)

6. Hector Hugh Munro, author of mischievous, witty and sometimes macabre stories that satirize Edwardian society and culture (4)

8. Eric Arthur Blair, 20th century British author and essayist, author of *Animal Farm* and *Nineteen Eighty-Four* (6, 6)

Down:

1. Dhanpat Rai Srivastav, one of India's greatest Hindi writers ever, whose best known novel was *Godaan* (6, 9)

2. Mary Westmacott, bestselling writer of murder mysteries, whose stage play *The Mousetrap* holds the record for the longest initial run (6, 8)

3. Charles Lutwidge Dodgson, creator of *Alice's Adventures in Wonderland* and *Through the Looking Glass* (5, 7)

5. Mary Ann Evans, author of *Mill on the Floss* and *Adam Bede*, an English Victorian novelist who adopted a man's name in order to escape gender-based prejudices among her readers (6, 5)

7. James Alfred ('Alf ') Wight, veterinary surgeon and author of works such as *All things Bright and Beautiful* and *All Creatures Great and Small* (5, 7)

Look Before You Leap

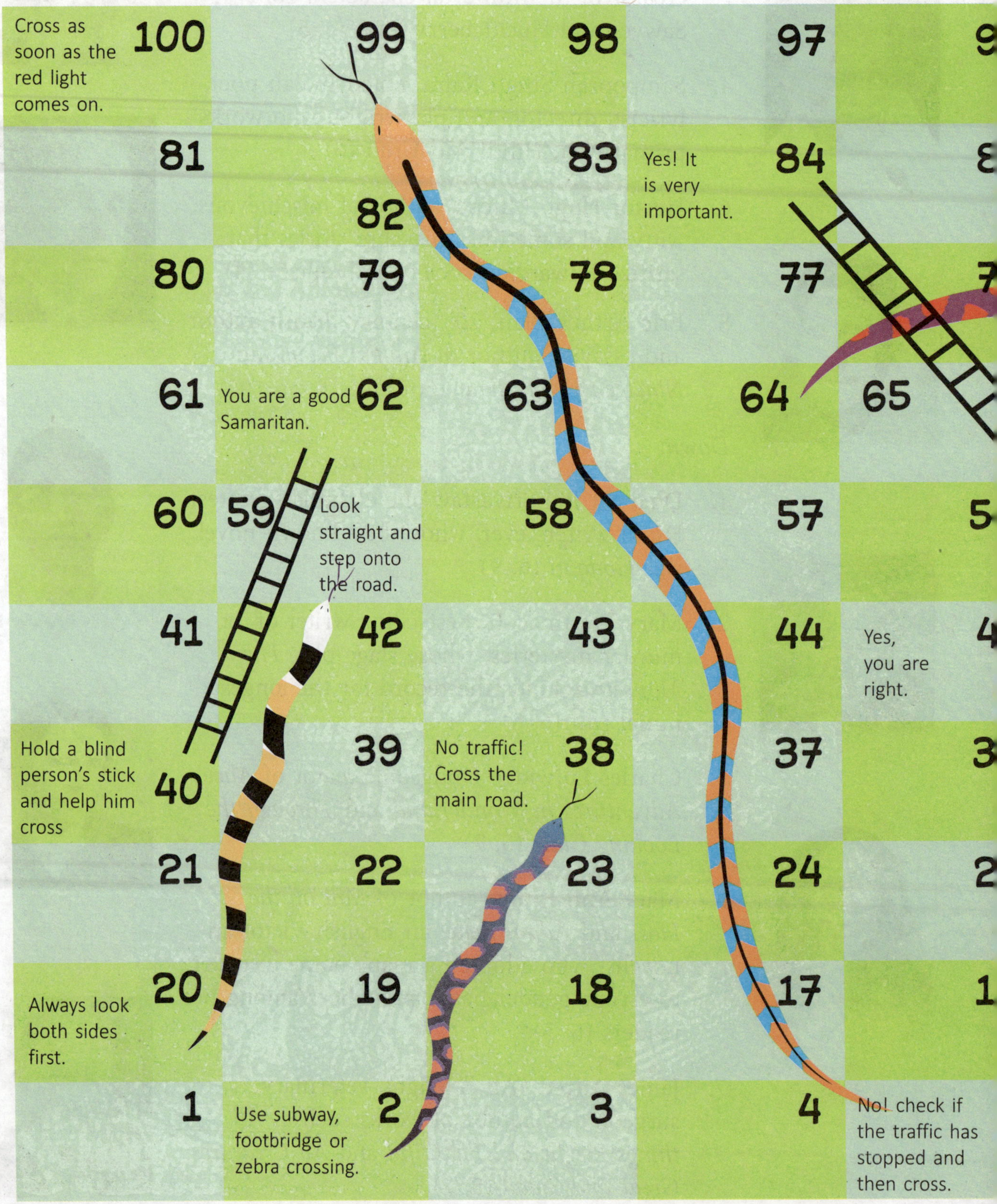

When you are walking on the pavement/crossing the road by foot, you are called a pedestrian. Play this game of snakes and ladders and see how many rules you know. Now roll the die and start playing.

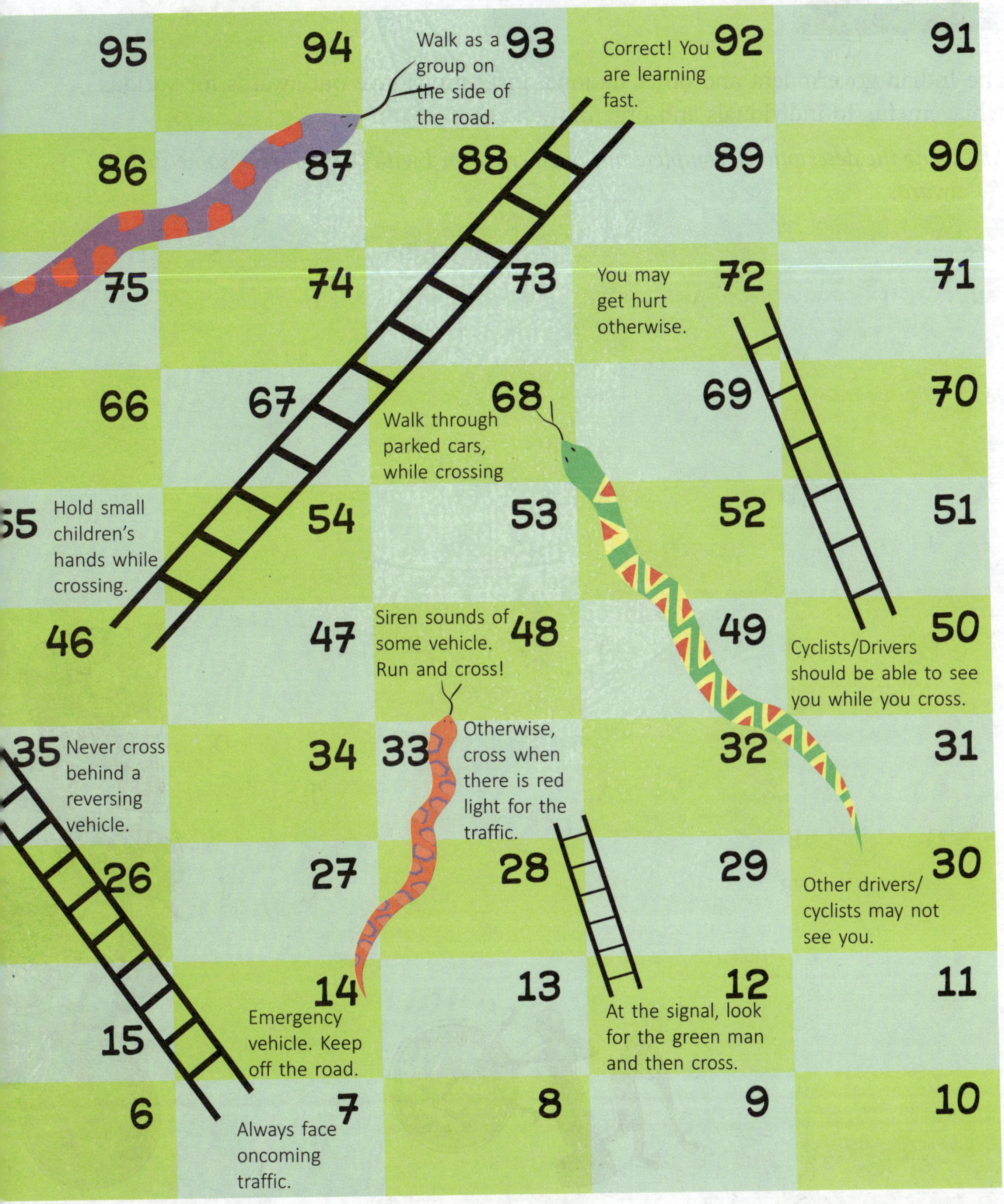

INDIA

16

Awards by the Indian Government

The Indian government and other national institutions give out awards for various achievements to individuals and organisations.

A. *Using the descriptions, complete this open crossword with the names of some such awards.*

Clues

Across

4. Honour given for the most spectacular and outstanding performance by an individual sportsperson or a team
8. India's highest award for lifetime achievement in sports and games named after a famous sports personality
10. Highest national award

Down

1. Outstanding performance in sports at national and international levels
2. Award given in the field of science
3. Award given for outstanding literary work
5. Highest sports award given to coaches for excellence in coaching
6. Outstanding contribution in the field of cinema
7. Prize given to individuals or organisations for promoting international peace and development
9. Award given to outstanding authors of creative literature

B. *Only three people have won all four Civilian Awards. Name these (1) singer, (2) instrumentalist, and (3) writer-musician-artist-filmmaker from their pictures.*

1. 

2. 

3. 

COOL FACT

Apart from the Bharat Ratna, there are three more civilian awards, together called the Padma Awards. They are, in order of increasing importance—the Padma Shri, the Padma Bhushan and the Padma Vibhushan. They are given to individuals (civilians) in recognition of exceptional service in any field of human endeavour.

Causes and Effects

Many of our day-to-day actions may be damaging to the environment. Some kinds of damage can be seen or felt immediately, while others are long term, which means their ill effects will be felt by all of us over several years.

A. *Below are the causes and effects of some common environment-unfriendly activities. Match the causes and effects.*

Causes	Effects
1. Television on high volume	a. Germs grow, leading to the spread of diseases
2. Cutting down trees	b. Chemical poisoning leading to air, water and soil pollution
3. Throwing garbage on the streets	c. Noise pollution
4. Throwing used batteries or tubelight into a kitchen dustbin	d. Soil erosion, less rainfall and drought
5. Washing clothes in rivers	e. Air pollution leading to greenhouse effect
6. Black smoke from vehicles and factories	f. Water pollution

B. *Read these statements and identify some major environmental disasters around the world. Choose their names from the help box.*

1. On December 3, 1984, at the Union Carbide pesticide plant, a poisonous gas called methyl iso-cyanate was accidentally released into the atmosphere, leading to the death of some ten thousand people and serious injuries to five lakh more people. ______________

2. ______________ On April 26, 1986, a major nuclear reactor meltdown occurred due to faulty design and operation at a nuclear power plant in what is present-day Ukraine.

3. On April 20, 2010, following an explosion and sinking of an oil rig, the largest and worst accidental marine oil spill took place in the Gulf of Mexico, massively affecting the environment. ______________

4. ______________ On March 11, 2011, three of the six nuclear reactors at a Japanese power plant shut down due to a major power failure and melt down, caused by a tsunami, resulting in radioactive contamination of the Japanese mainland.

5. In the 1960s, the USSR diverted the routes of Amu Darya and Syr Darya, the rivers that fed this water body, once the fourth largest lake in the world. By 2007, it had shrunk to ten per cent of its original size, making it one of the worst ecological disasters ever. ______________

6. ______________ Following the invasion of this Middle East country in 1991, the Iraqi military force blew up more than six hundred oil wells there. It took more than seven months to extinguish the well fires, causing one of the worst environmental disasters in the world.

The drying up of the Aral Sea	Bhopal Gas Tragedy	Chernobyl Nuclear Disaster
Kuwait Oil Fires	Fukushima Daiichi Nuclear Disaster	
Deepwater Horizon Oil Spill		

SAFETY SCIENCE

17

Electrical Safety

Electricity has revolutionised our lives. Think of what all gadgets we use that are powered by electricity! While it is very helpful, it can also cause nasty accidents if used incorrectly!

Here are some common questions you may have asked yourself or an adult. The answers are all given for you, but all jumbled up! Match the questions with their answers.

Questions	Answers
1. Why should you not stick your fingers, toys, etc. into electrical sockets?	a. Because water is a conductor of electricity. Water and electricity are a dangerous combination!
2. Why should you never place hair-dryers, radios and other electronic items near a bath tub or shower?	b. Because too many of them together could cause a surge of current and your different gadgets could get permanently damaged or even cause a fire!
3. Why should you not pull a plug from a socket by its cord?	c. Because if you touch a line by mistake, you could get a massive shock.
4. Why should you not climb trees near power lines?	d. Because electricity could jump out of the cord and give you a nasty shock!
5. Why should you not ever place glasses with drinks on video games, music players or other electronics?	e. Because they can spill, and when you touch that gadget, you could get zapped!
6. Why should you not plug multiple adapters one into another?	f. Because you can get an electric shock from the current flowing in the socket.

Some simple rules to avoid electrocution at home:

a. Always cover live sockets with a socket cover.
b. Never leave gaps or holes around electrical points.
c. Sockets in bathroom must always have covers.

Flag Maps

A flag-map is the outline map of a country with the national flag superimposed on it.

Here are flag maps of countries that have won the FIFA Football World Cup for men. Can you identify these countries?

1. 

Five time winners

2. 
The team is called The Azzurri

3. 
Won the 2014 World Cup

4. 
Home to Maradona and Messi

5. 
Won the First World Cup

6. 
Beckham and friends

7. 
Zidane's team

8. 
2010 Champions, home to the La Liga

Spain	France	England	Uruguay
Argentina	Germany	Italy	Brazil

COOL FACT

The first FIFA World Cup was held in Uruguay, South America because the country had won the Olympic Gold in football in the 1928 Amsterdam Games. Another reason for hosting the Cup was that Uruguay was celebrating the 100th anniversary of its constitution.

Children's Films

Fill in the blanks with the names of children's films listed in the help box.

1. Buzz Lightyear is an astronaut action figure who comes to life whenever humans are not present nearby. ______________
2. Simba returns to Pride Lands to challenge his evil uncle Scar who had killed his father Mufasa. ______________
3. Kevin McCallister is a young kid who is mistakenly left behind by his family when they fly to Paris for their Christmas vacation. ______________
4. Hiccup is a Viking teenager who lives in the remote island of Berk. He is supposed to slay a dragon named Toothless but instead he lets it live and they become friends. ______________
5. Marlin is a clownfish who resides in the Great Barrier Reef. With the help of Dory, he goes to Sydney Harbour to rescue his abducted son. ______________
6. *Edelweiss* and *Do-Re-Mi* are famous songs from a film which chronicles the musical lives of the von Trapp family. ______________

7. Professor Henry Higgins chose to teach a young woman selling flowers named Eliza Doolittle how to speak properly. ______________

8. Gru is a supervillain who seeks a loan from the Bank of Evil to execute his plan of shrinking and stealing the moon. ______________
9. A green ogre and his talking donkey are selected to rescue Princess Fiona, who is locked in a castle tower guarded by lava and a dragon. ______________
10. Bink is a mischievous baby belonging to a rich family. He gets kidnapped by three criminals. ______________
11. Princess Anna of Arendelle sets off on an adventure to find her sister Elsa, who possesses the unique power of being able to produce or create things with snow and ice. ______________

Despicable Me	*The Sound of Music*	*Shrek*	*Toy Story*
Finding Nemo	*Home Alone*	*The Lion King*	*My Fair Lady*
Frozen	*How to Train your Dragon*	*Baby's Day Out*	

COOL FACT *Beauty and the Beast* was the first animated film to be nominated for the Best Picture Oscar Award.

HISTORY

19

Story of the Automobile

Fill in the blanks using these clues about the history of the automobile. The missing words are given in the help box.

1. Today we cannot imagine a world without ____________. It is hard to imagine that just over 125 years ago there were no ____________ in our world.
2. Almost 250 years ago, a French army engineer, Nicolas-Joseph Cugnot, built the world's first 'automobile' which used a steam engine to pull large ____________ on the battlefield.
3. Then in 1807, the French inventor François Isaac de Rivaz, built a small automobile which had an engine that used ____________ and ____________ as fuels.
4. Interestingly in 1882, an Italian inventor, Enrico Bernardi, fitted a petrol engine in his son's ____________, thus making it the first automated vehicle with a petrol engine.
5. The first 'modern' automobile was built in 1886 by the German, Karl ____________. This car used petrol as fuel.
6. 1886 was a good year because the German inventors Gottlieb Daimler and Wilhelm Maybach also invented the first ____________ that year.
7. From this point onwards, hundreds of companies started manufacturing cars across the world. In 1908, ____________ manufactured the Model—T, which was the world's first affordable car.
8. The first company to manufacture cars in India was Hindustan Motors, whose best known car was the ____________.
9. Premier Auto started manufacturing cars as well, and was well-known for manufacturing the Premier ____________, named for a legendary Queen.
10. In the 1980s, the Maruti ____________, considered to be the first people's car, was launched by Maruti Suzuki.

SUZUKI

Benz	cars	cars	hydrogen	guns	800
oxygen	motorcycle	Ford	tricycle	Padmini	Ambassador

COOL FACT

The modern seat belt—called the three point seat belt—was invented by Volvo Engineer Nils Bohlin in 1959 and has saved millions of lives since then. Always wear a seat belt, whether you are in the front seat or at the back.

Tech Trivia

Each of these sets contain three items that have something in common. Choose what they have in common from the options given.

1. Rio, Space and Transformers are all editions of which game?
   a. Angry Birds b. Temple Run c. Subway Surfer
2. Alienware, XPS, Inspiron and Vostro are all PCs manufactured by which company?
   a. Dell b. HP c. HCL
3. X, G and E are all letters associated with mobile phones made by which company?
   a. Motorola b. Xiaomi c. Nokia
4. Lollipop, Froyo and Éclair are versions of which OS?
   a. Windows b. Android c. iOS
5. Fire, Voyage and Paperwhite are all versions of which product?
   a. Amazon Kindle b. Apple iPad c. Lenovo Yoga
6. Melissa, Brain and Stuxnet are all variations of what?
   a. Cookies b. Viruses c. Bugs
7. King, Imangi and Half Brick are all types of what?
   a. Computer games b. Music apps c. Mobile game studios
8. Xbox, Wii and Play Station are all examples of what?
   a. Music players b. Gaming consoles c. Home theatre systems
9. Vimeo, Metacafe and YouTube are all types of what?
   a. Browsers
   b. Video streaming websites
   c. Video downloaders
10. i7, i3 and i5 are all processors made by which company?
    a. INTEL
    b. AMD
    c. Apple

COOL FACT

In 2007, job applicant Jan Koum was rejected by Facebook as well as Twitter. So he started his own company. Seven years later, Facebook bought it for 19 billion dollars. The company was Whatsapp!

SCIENCE

21

An Acrostic on Space

Space is the final frontier. Look at these clues about celestial bodies and fill in the acrostic grid. Then find out if you have answered the final clue in the coloured column.

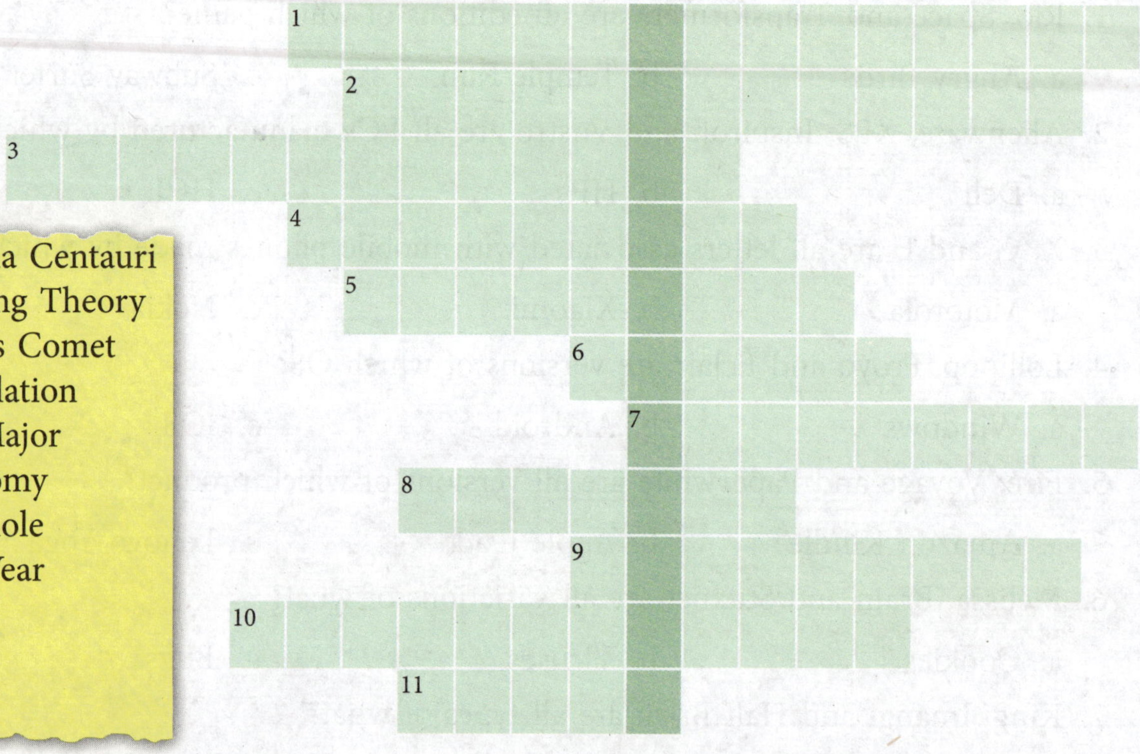

Proxima Centauri
Big Bang Theory
Halley's Comet
constellation
Ursa Major
astronomy
black hole
Light Year
Venus
Jupiter
galaxy

1. The star nearest to the sun
2. A group of stars identified with a pattern of animals or shapes
3. The theory which is the origin of the universe
4. A dead star that does not let light escape from it
5. Study of celestial bodies and the Universe
6. A huge collection of stars
7. A group of stars named *Great Bear* in Latin
8. Ganymede is the largest moon of this planet
9. Unit used to measure distances between stars and galaxies
10. The famous comet which appears every 76 years
11. Planet which is known as the twin of the Earth

Now check if the middle column matches this description.
The science of travel through air or space- ______________.

COOL FACT

Pluto was discovered in 1930 and named the ninth planet. But in 2006, the International Astronomical Union demoted it from planethood and classified it under a list of dwarf planets or plutoids.

LOGICAL REASONING

22

Closed Lists

A. *Given below are closed lists, which means all items that can fit into each list are there. Complete the lists using words from the options given next to each list. There are some extra incorrect options too.*

1. French, Australian, US and ____________ (Davis/Wimbledon/FIFA)
2. Rig, Yajur, ____________ and ____________ (Ayur/Sama/Chatur/Atharva)
3. Kada, Kesh, ____________, ____________ and ____________ (Kirpan/Kaagaz/Kanga/Kachehra/Kalam)
4. Babur, ____________, ____________, ____________, ____________ and Aurangzeb (Humayun/Akbar/Ibrahim Lodi/Jahangir/Hemu/Shah Jahan/Qutb-ud-din Aibak)
5. Delhi, ____________, A&N Islands, ____________, ____________, ____________ and ____________ (Goa/Puducherry/Daman & Diu/Jammu & Kashmir/Dadra and Nagar Haveli/Hyderabad/Chandigarh/Lakshadweep)
6. Bowled, Caught, LBW, Runout, Stumped, ____________, ____________, ____________, ____________ and ____________ (hit wicket/leg bye/handled the ball/hit the ball twice/boundary/obstructing the field/timed out/retired hurt/bogie)

B. *Now say what each list has in common. Use the help box below for the common labels.*

1. ________________________ 2. ________________________
3. ________________________ 4. ________________________
5. ________________________ 6. ________________________

Five Ks of Sikhism	Tennis Grand Slam tournaments
The Vedas	Ten ways of getting out in cricket
Seven Union Territories	Great Mughal Emperors

COOL FACT

Atyrau in Kazakhstan, Orenburg and Magnitogorsk in Russia, Suez in Egypt and Istanbul in Turkey form a closed list of five cities that are each spread over two continents. Four are spread over Asia and Europe, but only one straddles Asia and Africa. Can you guess which one?

23

Let's Visit France

We use more French words than we realise. Many French words are, in fact, used without an English translation. Such words are called loan words.

A. *Match these common French loan words with their meanings.*

French Loan words	Meanings
1. tête à tête	a. Perfume
2. en route	b. Eat well!
3. rouge	c. In the style of
4. Bon appétit!	d. Here you are!
5. Bon voyage!	e. Please reply
6. RSVP	f. Blusher
7. Café	g. On the way
8. eau de parfum	h. Have a happy journey!
9. à la…	i. A meeting of two people face to face
10. Voilà!	j. Canteen or mess that serves food and drinks

B. France has produced great names in different fields, from science to literature, philosophy to medicine, great art to popular culture.

In the following text, there are some cryptic clues connected with great French people underlined and numbered. Connect them with their names by putting the correct numbers next to the names.

Helen awoke this morning and had breakfast—a croissant with (a.) pasteurized butter. The kettle was connected to the five (b.) amps socket. She poured herself a cup of hot water and mixed in some chocolate.

The school walls were covered by the copies of famous (c.) Impressionists. In school, she studied (d.) Cartesian Geometry and elements like (e.) radium, curium and polonium. In Literature, she read, (f.) *Little Red Riding Hood and Beauty and the Beast*. In the afternoon, the class watched a (g.) film in the school auditorium. The film was (h.) *A Journey to the Centre of the Earth*. There was an interesting documentary before the main film about a (i.) code using raised dots as a reading aid for sightless people. In the evening, she read a story by Goscinny and Uderzo about a (j.) Gaul who fought the Romans.

1. André-Marie Ampère, electric current
2. Marie Curie, radioactivity
3. Lumière Brothers, cinema
4. Louis Pasteur, process of heating food to kill harmful microbes
5. Charles Perrault, fairy tales
6. Asterix, comic series
7. Jules Verne, science fiction
8. Louis Braille, writing code for the blind
9. Monet, Dégas, Renoir, XIX century artists
10. René Descartes, X and Y coordinates

Lumière Brothers

Louis Braille

Marie Curie

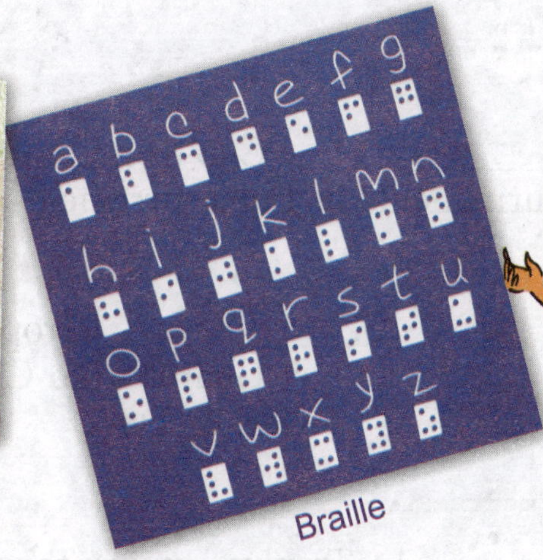

Braille

COOL FACT

Countries that use French as one of their official languages are called Francophone countries. These include Canada, Switzerland, many countries in Africa and East Asia. In India, Puducherry (formerly Pondicherry) uses French along with Tamil as an official language.

Indian Sporting Trophies

Can you identify the names of these sporting trophies of India using some letters of their names shown in each box? The coloured letter is the letter from which the names of the trophy starts

R	N
I	A

1. ____________ Trophy—domestic first-class cricket championship played between teams represented by regional cricket associations, services and railways

2. ______________ Trophy—national level cricket tournament for women where players represent regions and services like the five zones, Indian Railways and Air India.

R	S
I	A

S	O
N	A

3. __________ Trophy—football tournament which is played between teams representing Indian states and government institutions.

B	H
I	E

4. ______________ Cup—one of the oldest field Hockey tournaments in India, first held in Kolkata.

J	R
I	P

5. __________ Trophy—prestigious polo tournament, played at Guards Polo Club, that has been patronised by Rajmata Gayatri Devi.

6. __________ Trophy—racing tournament held amongst the famous snake boats on the Punnamda Lake, near Alappuzha, in Kerala.

E	N
U	R

COOL FACT

Durand Cup is named after the British diplomat Mortimer Durand. The international border between Pakistan and Afghanistan, called Durand Line, is also named after him. Durand Cup is the world's third oldest football tournament (after FA Cup and Scottish Cup) and Asia's oldest football tournament.

SPORTS

24

Martial Arts

This is Jackie Chan, one of the best known exponents of Martial Arts. Find the names of eight different martial arts in the word search below.

P	O	K	I	U	Y	T	R	E	W	Q	L	K
M	T	A	E	K	W	O	N	D	O	H	H	J
U	T	R	B	C	X	Z	A	S	D	F	G	J
A	Z	A	A	B	V	V	A	B	N	N	M	U
Y	I	T	U	O	Y	T	I	R	E	W	Q	J
T	K	E	N	D	O	H	K	U	N	G	F	U
H	K	H	T	U	N	K	I	Y	G	M	Z	T
A	W	E	R	J	T	Y	D	U	I	O	P	S
I	Q	W	E	R	T	V	O	N	M	R	T	U

COOL FACT

India has its own martial arts—one of which is *Kalaripayattu*, which originated in the state of Kerala and is practised even today.

25

Whales and Sharks

Whales and sharks have fascinated us since time immemorial and have been the subject of books, movies and folklore. How much do we really know about them?

A. *Try these quick quizzes about whales and sharks. Read the statements and write T for the True statements or F for the False statements in the space provided.*

WHALES		SHARKS	
1. They are the largest fish on earth.	☐	1. These are sea fish that eat meat.	☐
2. They are not hatched from eggs.	☐	2. They have many rows of sharp teeth.	☐
3. They breathe air through blowholes on top of their head.	☐	3. Their skeletons are made of bones.	☐
4. They swim by moving their tail from side to side.	☐	4. The gill slits are covered, like other fish.	☐
5. They are warm-blooded.	☐	5. Sharks can pick up electric signals of other animals.	☐
6. The blue whale is the biggest animal that ever lived.	☐	6. Sharks give birth to live young.	☐

B. *Now find as many whales and sharks as you can in the word search. You have been given some clues about them below as extra information.*

1. _______________ has tough bristles hanging inside its mouth. It uses these to sieve its food from water.
2. _______________ dives over two kilometres after its food.
3. _______________ can leap high into the air, turn somersaults in the air and dive back into the water.
4. _______________ swims long distances for food in summer (to colder regions) and in winter (to warmer regions).
5. _______________ is only ten centimetres long.
6. _______________ can swim at the speed of seventy-five kilometres per hour. That is really fast!
7. _______________ pumps water over its gills, so it spends most of its time on the seabed, without moving.

8. ________________ has a hammer-shaped head. Upto forty hammerhead shark pups may be born in one litter.

9. ____________ eats anything, ranging from paper, tin cans, plastic, tyres to people.

10. ________________ has a long tail that is often longer than its main body. It uses the tail to stun fish or to round them up.

W	A	S	D	F	G	P	N	B	M	I	Y	V	W	T	H
O	T	H	R	E	S	H	E	R	S	H	A	R	K	Q	A
B	I	Z	Y	O	M	Q	S	P	D	L	H	J	B	B	M
B	G	R	E	Y	W	H	A	L	E	V	S	Y	P	A	M
E	E	R	T	W	Q	M	B	C	X	Z	Y	U	I	S	E
G	R	E	A	T	W	H	I	T	E	S	H	A	R	K	R
O	S	P	O	S	T	G	F	D	S	A	L	K	J	I	H
N	H	U	M	P	B	A	C	K	W	H	A	L	E	N	E
G	A	N	G	E	L	S	H	A	R	K	T	Y	U	G	A
S	R	N	U	R	S	E	S	H	A	R	K	B	P	S	D
H	K	P	O	M	U	Y	T	R	E	T	M	B	N	H	S
A	R	T	D	W	A	R	F	S	H	A	R	K	G	A	H
R	Y	U	I	H	N	B	V	R	O	P	A	S	D	R	A
K	F	G	M	A	K	O	S	H	A	R	K	H	I	K	R
S	W	E	L	L	S	H	A	R	K	S	G	L	K	J	K
V	B	A	L	E	E	N	W	H	A	L	E	X	B	N	R

11. ________________, also known as White Death, can swallow whole seals and sea lions in one go.

12. ________________ spends a lot of time at the ocean's surface on sunny days.

13. ________________ or monkfish has very large pectoral fins, just like an angel's wings. It spends most of its time on the ocean floor.

14. ________________ can disguise itself on the seabed with its colouring, marking and seaweed-like structures around its mouth.

15. ________________, when attacked by a predator, swells up like a balloon by gulping down lot of sea water and hide itself inside a crack in a rock.

COOL FACT The whale shark is not a whale but a shark. It is the biggest of all fish, measuring fifteen metres in length.

Stamp Collecting

Stamps are a great way to learn about the history and culture of its people. The world's first postage stamp was issued in the United Kingdom in 1840 and is called the Penny Black. In 1852, the Scinde Dawk became the first stamp to be issued in India.

Philately is the collection or study of stamps. Philatelists study stamps, postal stationery, postal history, perforation (that is the row of little dots along which you tear out a stamp from the sheet), seals and markings and even the gum used to stick stamps to envelopes.

This is a stamp that honours Mahatma Gandhi, which was issued by the United Kingdom in 1969. Like all UK stamps, it does not mention the name of the country. Do you know why?

Most countries have their names on their postage stamps. Many are in English as well as their own language. So examining stamps of different countries is a good way to learn their local names.

A. *Look at these stamps. See how information can be derived at by just looking at them.*

Picture of the stamp	Name in local language	Name of the country
1. 	Suomi	Finland
2. 	Suid Afrika	South Africa
3. 	مصر	Egypt

B. Some stamps do not bear the name of the country in English, but by looking carefully at the image on the stamp and the name of the country in the local language, you can guess the country. Can you guess which countries have issued the following stamps?

Picture of the stamp	Clue	Name of the country in English
1. 	World's longest defensive wall	____________
2. 	Alfred Nobel	____________
3. 	Leaning Tower of Pisa	____________
4. 	A large football playing country	____________
5. 	Bull Fighting	____________
6. 	Stars and the Stripes	____________
7. 	A multipurpose knife	____________

AROUND THE WORLD

26

Bridges

All of us are fascinated by bridges. Bridges allow us to travel over water or other obstacles. Bridges are of different types. Some of them are given below.

beam bridge

truss bridge

cantilever bridge

arch bridge

suspension bridge

cable stayed bridge

COOL FACT India's tallest bridge is being built across the Chenab river in Jammu and Kashmir with a height of 359 metres. When completed, it will allow trains to travel from Jammu to Srinagar.

Fill in the missing information about some world-famous bridges in this table. But watch out! There are three extra answers.

	Description	Place
 ________________	The bridge deck folds upwards to allow ships to pass through.	London, UK
 Millau Viaduct	The ______________ bridge in the world (343 metres tall)	Millau, France
 Iron Bridge	First iron bridge in the world was completed in 1779	Shropshire, ______________
 Golden Gate Bridge	The largest suspension bridge was built in 1937.	______________, USA
 Sydney Harbour Bridge	Known as the ______________, it is a rail, road, cycle and pedestrian bridge.	Sydney, Australia
 ________________	First bridge across the Grand Canal of Venice	Venice, Italy

England	Tower Bridge	longest	tallest	San Francisco
Rialto	Coathanger	Los Angeles	Ponte Vecchio	London Bridge

27

Folk Dances of North East India

The North East is a culturally diverse and vibrant region, and nowhere is this aspect so beautifully and evocatively expressed than in their folk dances.

Solve the rebus/cryptic clues to get the names and fill in the crossword boxes. Then read the descriptions to get a real feel of each dance form!

REBUS/CRYPTIC CLUES

ACROSS

3. nickname for a revolutionary leader of Cuba + acronym of the Research and Analysis Wing (3+3=6)
6. Popular Sikh title or surname for men + I, CH +  ham (5+1, 2+3=6, 5)
8. A word to express gratitude – KS + G, half of one of India's biggest industrial houses (5+2=7)

DOWN

1.  bag + U + (a rhythmic dance from Cuba, with Spanish and African elements) (4+5=9)
2. 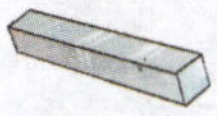 bar + (first note in western music), CH +  ham (3+2, 2+3=5, 5)
4. A part of Santa Claus' laugh + "Yes" in German + a traditional Sanskrit word for mountain (think Nil-, Sapta-, Dhaula- (2+2+4=8)
5. A prefix for "two" or "both" + synonym for colour – E (2+2=4)
7. Tintin's Chinese Friend/Jackie ______ G + interjection ______ and behold! (5, 2)

Description

3. A mesmerising combination of rhythm and skill, the dance has four people holding two pairs of long bamboos across one another on the ground. As the bamboo sticks are clapped together, the main dancers in traditional attire weave patterns through them in time to the rhythm.

6. A masked dance of Sikkim, depicting the snow lion – the cultural symbol of the state. The dancers display their cultural symbol by dressing up in furry costumes and performing this majestic masked dance.

8. This is more like a martial art of Manipur. It is called Huyen Langlon in Manipuri. The weapons used, including sword, spear, dagger are combined with the practice of controlling the self. With the rhythm of breathing, soft movements are done by expert dancers.

1. A folk dance considered the main traditional dance of the Bodo tribe. It is accompanied by musical instruments like kham (a long drum, made of wood and goat skin or other animal's skin), sifung (flute), jota (made of iron/tama), serja (bowed instrument, made of wood and animal skin), gongwna (made of bamboo) and tharkha (a piece of split bamboo).

2. This folk dance depicts the victory of good over evil. According to local beliefs, forces — both good and evil, rule mankind. In one year, twelve different types of stupid things representing evil forces are said to appear each month. The Sherdukpens mask themselves representing different animals and dance to the accompaniment of drums.

4. A reflection of the age-old culture and unique style of dance of the Reang community of Tripura, in this dance, only the lower half of the body is moved to create rhythmic movements. Dancers perform amazing acrobatic feats, including dancing on an earthen pitcher or balancing a bottle on the head with a lighted lamp on top.

5. This folk dance from Assam is related to the festival of the same name. Performed by both young men and women, it is characterised by brisk dance steps and rapid hand movements. Female dancers wear mekhala-chador while male dancers put on dhoti-gamocha in the dance performance. Dhol (drum), Pepa (Horn), Baahi (flute), Gagana (made of bamboo) are the instruments used.

7. Also known as Sua Lua, this is a dance of a Nagaland tribe. It was performed to celebrate the victory over enemies in the earlier times and now forms a part of all community celebrations, such as Poanglem, a three-day festival preceding the harvest season. There are dramatic costumes of the traditional Naga warrior and finery of womenfolk.

Classification of Books

There are thousands of books in a library. Unless the books are properly classified, they will get lost. An American librarian named Melvil Dewey devised a popular classification system that divides books into ten main groups.

A. *Here is a colourful bar chart of the books in a school library. Each bar represents the type of books belonging to each subject category and its respective code.*

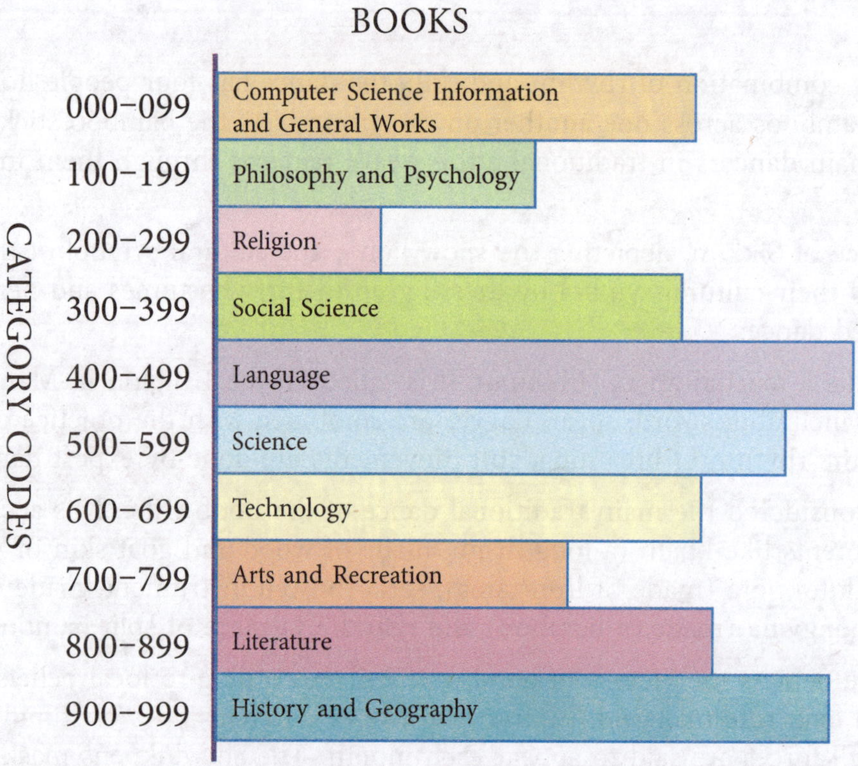

Now look at the list of books given below and write the category and code next to the book name. One has been done for you.

List of books	Category Code
1. *Collins English Dictionary and Thesaurus*	000-099
2. *Windows to World Religions* by Arvind Sharma	
3. *Mastering French Vocabulary* (Barron's Foreign Language Guides) by Wolfgang von Fischer, Anne-Marie Le Plouhinec	
4. *A Concise Textbook of Human Psychology* by Dr Sarabjeet Kaur	

5. *Oil & Acrylic: Land and Sea: Learn to Paint Step by step* (How to Draw & Paint) by Vernon Kerr	
6. *Rivers of India* by Radhakant Bharati	
7. *The Art of Computer Programming* by Donald E Knuth	
8. *Humanities and Social Science* by Prof Madhavi Pradhan, Prof Swapnaja Hirai and Prof. Nitin Shekapure	
9. *Science in Seconds for Kids* by Jean Potter	
10. *Textbook of Agricultural Biotechnology* by Nag Ahindra	
11. *Adventures of Huckleberry Finn* by Mark Twain	
12. *Production Technology* (Manufacturing Process) by PC Sharma	
13. *UNIX - Concepts and Applications* by Sumitabha Das	
14. *Modern Children's Literature - An Introduction* by Kimberley Reynolds (Editor)	
15. *History of Modern India* by Bipan Chandra	
16. *Landmark Integrated Social Sciences 6-8* by Indira Subramanian and Ramesh Mathur	
17. *An Introduction to Indian Music* by B Chaitanya	
18. *Sachin—Cricketer of the Century* by Vimal Kumar	
19. *The Story of Philosophy* by Will Durant	
20. *Paradise Lost* by John Milton	

Congratulations! You have now classified the books into different sections, as in a library.

B. *Now, try to classify the books that you own and arrange them in your bookcase under different categories and codes. Write the name of the book, the category to which it belongs and the appropriate code. This will help you to organise your own library.*

COOL FACT

Under the Delivery of Books and Newspapers (Public Libraries) Act, 1954, a copy of every book published in India must be sent to each of the following libraries – National Library in Kolkata, Delhi Public Library, Connemara Public Library in Chennai and the State Central Library in Mumbai.

TRIVIA

28

World Trivia

There are more than two hundred countries in the world. Let us have some fun with their names.

A. *All these countries have 'land' in their names. Read the clues and guess their names.*

1. A land that was the country of origin of the famous scientist Marie Curie.

   ____

2. A land famous for its beautiful landscape, cuckoo clocks and chocolates.

   ____

3. A land where Santa Claus is supposed to live in the village of Rovaniemi.

   ____

4. Lands whose name means 'low-lying', famous for its tulip fields

   ____

5. A land near the United Kingdom whose capital is Dublin.

   ____

6. A small land in Africa near South Africa and Mozambique

   ____

7. A cold volcanic land in the middle of the North Atlantic Ocean

   ____

8. A cricket-playing land near Australia

   ____

B. *Rearrange these letters and add 'stan' to get the names of seven countries.*

1. KKAHAZ ______________________
2. TMNIRUKE ______________________
3. TIIJKA ______________________
4. UEKIBZ ______________________
5. KZRYYG ______________________
6. PIAK ______________________
7. AINFHAG ______________________

C. *Fill in the blanks using words from the help box to get the names of four countries with a 'direction' in their name.*

1. East ______________________
2. South ______________________
3. Central ______________________
4. South ______________________

Sudan
Africa
Timor
African Republic

Cool Activity 1

There is only one country each whose name begins with an O, Q or Y. Can you find them? Find them and write their names here.

a. ______________________

b. ______________________

c. ______________________

Cool Activity 2

Groups of countries are sometimes referred to together by a single name or acronyms. Here are some of the group names. Find out the names of all the countries that form a part of the group. To help you, we have given you the number of countries within brackets.

a. Benelux (3)

b. Anzac (2)

c. Iberia (2)

d. Scandinavia (5)

COOL FACT There are no countries whose names begin with 'W' or 'X'.

29

Olympic Superheroes

Complete the statements about Olympic superheroes and their achievements. Each statement has four blanks. Choose the four correct options from the given options.

1. The ____________ swimmer, Michael ____________ won a ____________ of eighteen gold medals, two silver medals and two ____________ medals at the Olympic Games.

   Options: *total, silver, bronze, US, Jackson, Phelps*

2. ____________ Oerter won the discus ____________ at four ____________ Olympics from ____________ to 1968.

   Options: *throw, 1956, Al, put, 1960, consecutive*

3. The ____________ athlete, Paavo Nurmi, also known as the '____________ Finn', won nine gold and ____________ silver medals in his ____________ career.

   Options: *three, Finnish, Flying, Olympic, gymnastics, bronze*

4. In ____________, Jesse Owens became the first ____________ to win four ____________ medals in athletics at one edition of the Olympic ____________.

   Options: *Games, cups, cricketer, 1936, person, gold*

5. The American ____________, Carl Lewis, ____________ nine gold medals from 1984 to 1996. He won the long jump gold at four ____________ Olympics—1984, 88, ____________ and 96.

   Options: *92, single, athlete, won, 90, consecutive*

6. The ______________ gymnast, Larisa ______________ won eighteen Olympic medals from 1956 to 1964, a ____________ that was broken only in ______________.

Options: *Indian, 2008, Latynina, 1966, Soviet, record*

7. The US Swimmer Mark Spitz won seven gold medals in the 1972 ______________ Games and broke the existing world ______________ in each ____________ that he participated in. He was nicknamed '______________ the Shark'.

Options: *event, New Delhi, Mark, Michael, Munich, record*

8. ______________ Comaneci, the Romanian gymnast won five Olympic ______________ and also scored a perfect ______________ in the 1976 ______________ Olympics.

Options: *Summer, Nadia, gold medals, twenty, winter, ten*

9. The British ______________ Steve ______________ is the ______________ person to have won a gold medal at ______________ consecutive Olympic Games—from 1984 to 2000.

Options: *cricketer, Redgrave, five, rower, four, only*

10. Two Indian ______________ players have won three Olympic gold medals as well as an Olympic ____________; they are Leslie ____________ and ______________ Singh.

Options: *football, silver, gold medals, Udham, Claudius, hockey*

COOL FACT Philip Noel-Baker is the only person to have won an Olympic medal (Silver in athletics at the 1920 Antwerp Olympics) as well as a Nobel Prize (for Peace in 1959).

NATURAL WORLD

30

Strange-Looking Animals

Not all creatures are cute or cuddly. Nature also has some strange-looking animals.

Given below are the pictures, the names of the animals and the place where they are found. Match them.

1. Proboscis		a. Turtle	i. Island of Borneo
2. Titicaca		b. Dog	ii. Lake Titicaca
3. Pig-nosed		c. Monkey	iii. Found in northern Australia, Irian, Jaya and Southern New Guinea
4. British		d. Water Frog	iv. United Kingdom
5. Crested Hairless		e. Bat	v. China

6. Celestial-Eyed 	f. Condor	vi. China, Korea
7. Star nosed 	g. Mole Rat	vii. Eastern North America
8. Sphynx 	h. Gold Fish	viii. Canada
9. Naked 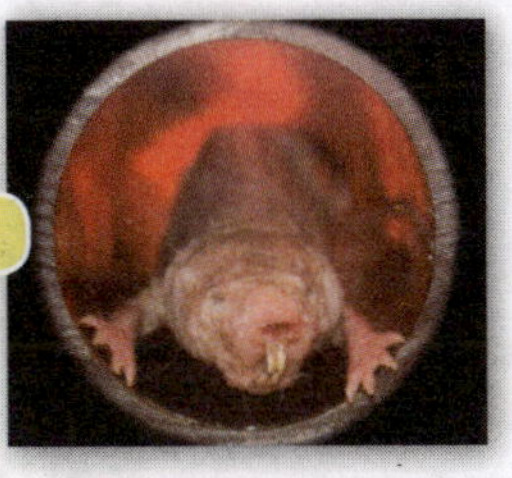	i. Mole	ix. East African Deserts
10. California 	j. Cat	x. North America

COOL FACT

The Blobfish, found in the marine waters of the Atlantic, Indian and Pacific oceans, is a deep sea creature. The poor thing has been consistently voted the world's ugliest animal year after year.

INDIA

31

Indian Classical Instrumentalists

India has produced some fine musicians proficient at playing different instruments.

Look at the images of these famous musicians playing their instruments of choice and complete the statements.

1. Zakir Hussain is an accomplished ____________ player.

2. Pandit Ravi Shankar was the most famous exponent of the ________ ever, having worked with several international musicians and also a composer of many ragas.

3. N Ramani is a __________ following the Carnatic music tradition.

4. Pandit Shivkumar Sharma plays the melodious __________ and is also a music composer.

5. Ustad Amjad Ali Khan and his sons, Ayaan Ali Khan and Amaan Ali Khan, are well-known __________ players.

6. E Gayathri is a famous ________ player.

7. Hariprasad Chaurasia is a composer of international repute. He plays the __________.

8. Palghat Mani Iyer is a well-known __________ player.

9. U Srinivas was a very gifted __________ player who died in 2014.

10. TH Vinayakram plays the special earthen pot called the __________.

11. L Subramaniam is an internationally renowned ______________ .

12. Ustad Bismillah Khan was one of the best __________ players of all times.

tabla	violinist	flautist	santoor
sarod	veena	flute	ghatam
mandolin	shehnai	sitar	mridangam

COOL FACT

Rudra, Chitra, Vichitra, Hansa, Mohan and Saraswati, Ranjan, Triveni are some prefixes for different types of the same basic musical instrument: the Veena, one of the ancient musical instruments of India, mentioned in the *Vedas* as well as the *Natyashastra*.

MI

Dances of the World

A. *Find the names of eighteen popular dance forms from around the world in this word search.*

A	H	I	P	H	O	P	B	T	Y	B	E	L	L	F	A
C	O	E	J	L	S	C	P	K	O	Q	S	U	A	G	J
D	P	F	I	P	A	J	O	Z	C	B	S	A	M	B	A
S	A	L	S	A	D	N	L	M	H	D	F	H	B	F	Z
G	K	H	Q	H	P	R	K	C	A	G	I	K	A	H	Z
K	M	R	D	I	T	C	A	N	C	A	N	G	D	E	K
N	O	V	R	Y	J	L	O	S	H	B	I	F	A	J	L
U	S	X	A	V	M	F	T	W	A	Z	O	L	X	Y	M
T	A	N	G	O	N	O	U	D	C	P	R	A	N	W	Z
W	M	R	O	V	A	X	Q	S	H	T	U	M	D	A	G
Z	A	Q	N	V	X	T	A	R	A	N	T	E	L	L	A
A	N	Y	D	W	B	R	J	M	O	Q	U	N	Y	T	X
C	F	W	A	X	S	O	D	O	R	I	Z	C	A	Z	D
V	K	S	N	I	N	T	W	E	G	J	C	O	T	L	Q
B	R	L	C	F	I	K	M	O	R	U	W	A	I	D	V
H	P	B	E	L	L	Y	D	A	N	C	E	N	P	S	T

B. *Look at these pictures of dancers.*

Tango

Hip Hop

Bon Odori

Dragon Dance

Now answer these questions.

1. I like the picture of ____________________ because of
   a. the dancer's pose.
   b. the dancer's costume.
   c. the props used for this dance form.

Flamenco

2. Do you like dance?
   a. No. b. Yes.

   If no, why?
   i. I have two left feet.
   ii. It tires me out.
   iii. I prefer sports.
   iv. I prefer singing or playing an instrument without moving.
   v. I am scared of performing on the stage.

   If yes, what do you like about dance?
   i. I love moving to fast music.
   ii. I love the beautiful dance costumes.
   iii. I love being on the stage.
   iv. I like to choreograph moves.

Salsa

3. a. Which of the dance forms in the word search have you heard of?

   ____

   b. Which one/s do you like? Say why, in the space given below.

   ____

Let's Visit South Africa

Try this quick quiz on one of the world's most vibrant countries—South Africa. The answers are in the help box.

1. The South African government recognizes how many official languages?

   ____

2. South Africa has three capitals. If Pretoria is the executive capital and Bloemfontein is the judicial capital, then what is the legislative capital?

   ____

3. Africa's only endemic penguins can be found in parts of South Africa. Write their name, which is based on the donkey-like braying of the males?

   ____

4. Nelson Mandela was elected as the first coloured president of South Africa, after being imprisoned for almost twenty-eight years resisting ____________________.

5. In which island, now a UNESCO world heritage site, was Nelson Mandela imprisoned for eighteen years?

   ____

6. Which famous South African landmark is flanked by Devil's Peak to the east and by Lion's Head to the west?

   ____

7. The famous Portuguese explorer, Bartolomeu Dias, originally gave what name to the Cape of Good Hope?

   ____

8. Abraham Benjamin are the initial names of which famous South African cricketer? ______________

9. With which major sporting event held in South Africa would you associate the names 'Zakumi', 'Jabulani' and 'Waka Waka'? ______________

10. ____________ National Park is one of the largest game reserves in Africa and South Africa's first national park. ______________

11. Afrikaans is one of the most important official languages of South Africa. Which European language is it derived from? ______________

12. The King ____________ is the national flower of South Africa. The flower lends its name to the nickname of the South African national cricket team.

13. Nadine Gordimer and JM Coetzee are two of the most famous ______________ from South Africa.

____

14. Cullinan, also called the Great Star of Africa was found in a mine in Pretoria, South Africa in 1905. What is it? ______________

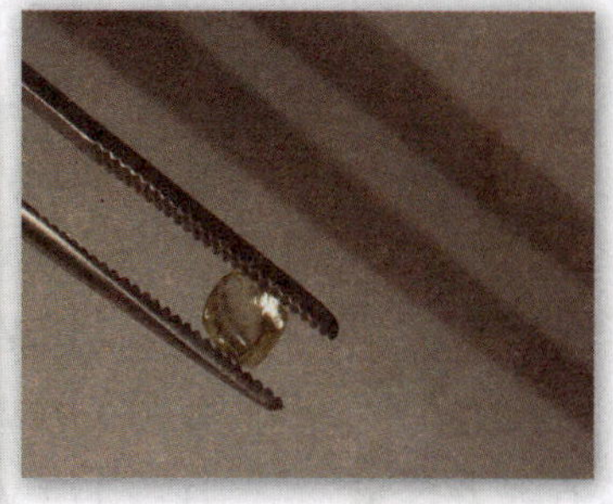

Cape Town	Cape of Storms	Jackass Penguins
Apartheid	Table Mountain	Robben Island
de Villiers	Kruger	Protea
Dutch	Diamond	authors/writers
Eleven	2010 FIFA World Cup	

COOL FACT

Cradle of Humankind is a UNESCO world heritage site that is situated in the Gauteng province of South Africa. It was named so because the site has been the centre of a large number of, as well as some of the oldest, hominin fossils ever found, some dating back as far as 3.5 million years ago.

33

Common Insects

Match three statements about each common insect with its picture and name by writing the correct numbers in the circles.

1.  Ants ◯ ◯ ◯

2.  Ladybirds ◯ ◯ ◯

3.  Silverfish ◯ ◯ ◯

4.  Cicadas ◯ ◯ ◯

5.  Termites ◯ ◯ ◯

6.  Wasps ◯ ◯ ◯

a. The bright colours warn birds that they do not taste good.
b. They live in colonies where there are workers, soldiers, a king and a queen.
c. The buzzing and the clicking noises made by a group grows into an overpowering hum.
d. The spots on them fade as they get older.
e. Some produce loud noisy calls that can be heard upto 1.5 kms away.
f. Some species of these insects disappear entirely for many years and then reappear in force, at regular intervals.
g. They rest but never sleep.
h. They are used for controlling pests as they feed on them.
i. They can lift objects fifty times heavier than themselves.
j. They live together in special homes called nests.
k. The rooms of their many dwellings are called galleries.
l. They feed on damp wood, plaster, paint, etc., and are capable of destroying buildings or trees.
m. These small wingless insects have two long antennae and they wiggle like a fish.
n. They love to consume starchy items like glue, book bindings, clothing, paper, etc.
o. They can run very swiftly and can outpace most of their predators.
p. They create their familiar papery abodes from wood fibers.
q. They come in every colour imaginable, from the familiar yellow to brown, metallic blue and bright red.
r. You can tell the difference between them and bees by their pointed lower abdomens and the narrow waist.

COOL FACT

While many insects, such as honeybees, mosquitoes and flies, use their feelers to hear, some have peculiar ears. The grasshopper has its eardrum in its abdomen, while the male locust hears with a large thin membrane inside its rear leg joint.

TRIVIA

34

Everyday Inventions

Read these statements that explain how some of these inventions for the home, work. Based on the statements, write the names of the devices. Then match them with their pictures.

1. Pictures are captured by cameras, turned into waves and sent out. These waves are caught by receivers, called antennae, and converted back into picture form by picture tubes and more recently, liquid crystals at the receiving end. John Logie Baird is officially credited with its invention. ______________

2. Sound vibrations at one end are changed into electric patterns that travel over wire and get reconverted to sound vibrations at the receiver's end. Originally credited to Alexander Graham Bell, today Italian Antonio Meucci is considered the rightful inventor of this device. ______________

3. Its two main parts are the condenser at the top, which removes heat and makes the air cooler inside and the compressor, which converts gas to liquid and expels the heat. The modern version of this appliance is based on the ideas developed by Oliver Evans and Jacob Perkins. ______________

4. Hot air is sucked in from the surroundings, passed through a compressor, where it gets squeezed to liquid form and the heat is taken out. Willis Carrier is credited with its invention. ______________

5. This invention by Hubert Booth was used on the ceremonial carpet for King Edward VII's coronation. It sucks in dust particles from all surfaces. ______________

6. This invention started as a scrub board, this invention became a hand powered drum, improvised as a rotary machine and then was designed and gifted as a convenient home-run machine. So many people worked to make it perfect that just one inventor cannot be named. ______________

COOL FACT

This is how the first wireless TV remote control looked like. It was called the Flash-matic. It used a light beam to send signals to receptors on a TV set.

Mnemonics

A mnemonic is a learning technique that helps us in memorising things very easily. The word comes from the Greek word mnēmōn that means 'mindful'.

A. *There are many different kinds of mnemonics that you can use depending on how you prefer to learn. Read them and match them with the examples.*

Name	Description	Example
1. Name Mnemonics	The first letter of each word of the group is used to remember all the words.	a. Do-re-mi
2. Expression or Word Mnemonic	The first letter of each word in the mnemonic stands for the items in a group in the right order.	b. I before E except after C or when sounding like A as in neighbour and weigh.
3. Image Mnemonic	An image is used to remember difficult things.	c. VIBGYOR
4. Music Mnemonics	Song lyrics help us learn better than plain texts.	d. Using the bumps and gaps in knuckles to remember the number of days in each month
5. Spelling Mnemonics	A sentence that can help you remember the spelling of a word.	e. My very educated mother just served us noodles (to learn the names of the planets in order).
6. Connection Mnemonics	To remember something new, we can connect it with something we already know.	f. A person can be a PAL, like my school princiPAL.
7. Rhyme or Ode Mnemonics	A rhyme or a poem can help us remember things.	g. Learning dates by matching them with birthdays, phone numbers or other familiar information.

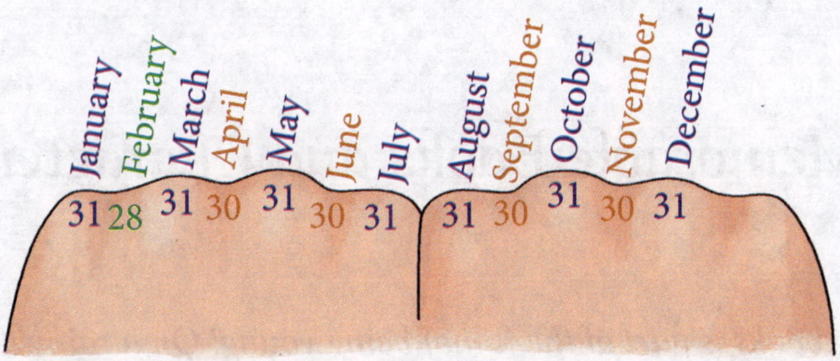

B. *Now answer these questions using the mnemonics that work for you.*

How do you normally remember information or lists?

1. image
2. music, song or rhyme
3. connections
4. name or word mnemonics

C. *Which mnemonic would you use to remember them from the list below?*

1. Please Let Harry Scare The Massive Cat
2. PL-HS-TMC
3. Tetrapak, oblong, leaves, person, temple, coffin, huge person
4. Pyramids, Lighthouse, Hanging Gardens;
   Zeus, Artemis, Mausoleum;
   And don't forget the Colossus then;
   That's the complete Wonders Rhyme!
5. I go from Cairo to Alexandria, passing by the gardens, taking a picture with my friend Zeus, praying in the temple of Artemis, leaving a bouquet by the Mausoleum and meeting a Rhodes scholar under the Colossus!

D. *The Seven Wonders of the Ancient World are—*

1. Pyramids at Giza
2. Lighthouse at Alexandria
3. Hanging Gardens of Babylon
4. Statue of Zeus
5. Temple of Artemis
6. Mausoleum at Halicarnassus
7. Colossus of Rhodes

E. *How would you remember the differences between these?*

1. Latitude and Longitude
2. Stalactites and Stalagmites

F. *Here is a mnemonic. What does it help you remember?*

My New English Madam offered no individual coaching

LANGUAGE AND LITERATURE

35

Memorable Books and Characters

A. *The thrill of reading books is part of the fun of being young! On a rainy day or on a train journey, try reading one of these books. Can you match them with their authors?*

a.

Lewis Carroll

b.

Roald Dahl

c.

Charles Dickens

d.

JK Rowling

e.

RK Narayan

f.

JM Barrie

g.

RL Stevenson

h.

Suzanne Collins

i.

L Frank Baum

j.

Antoine de Saint-Exupéry

1. *Harry Potter and the Philosopher's Stone*
2. *Charlie and the Chocolate Factory*
3. *The Little Prince*
4. *Swami and Friends*
5. *Treasure Island*
6. *Peter Pan*
7. *Oliver Twist*
8. *Hunger Games*
9. *Wizard of Oz*
10. *Alice's Adventures in Wonderland*

B. *Here is one statement about each of these books with one or two key words missing. Fill in the blanks with the words given in the box below.*

Oliver Twist	Hearts	Dursley	island	Malgudi	Tributes
Little Prince	Dorothy	treasure	Neverland	Willy Wonka	

1. 'Off with her head!' is what the Queen of __________ said in '*Alice in Wonderland*'.
2. 'Please sir, I want some more', said __________ __________, a poor orphan boy.
3. Swami lived with his friends in a small town in South India called __________.
4. Jim Hawkins was a boy who went to sea in the *Hispaniola* and found a __________ on an __________ which made him rich for life!
5. __________ was the little girl who went to meet the Wizard of Oz with her companions—the Tin Man, the Scarecrow and the Lion.
6. __________ __________ owned a chocolate factory which made the best chocolates in the world.
7. Number 4, Privet Drive, Little Whinging, Surrey is where the __________ family lived.
8. __________ was the magical island where Peter Pan and the Lost Boys lived.
9. The eponymous Hunger Game in the novel is a televised event where the participants are called __________.
10. The __________ __________ is a kid who falls to Earth and meets a pilot stranded in the desert.

COOL FACT

In the famous novel *Robinson Crusoe*, Friday was Crusoe's friend and servant. He was called so because Crusoe met him on a friday. The character is the source of the well-known expression Man Friday.

36

Sources of Energy

A. *Match the kind of power with the pictures and the source of power.*

1.

2.

3.

4.

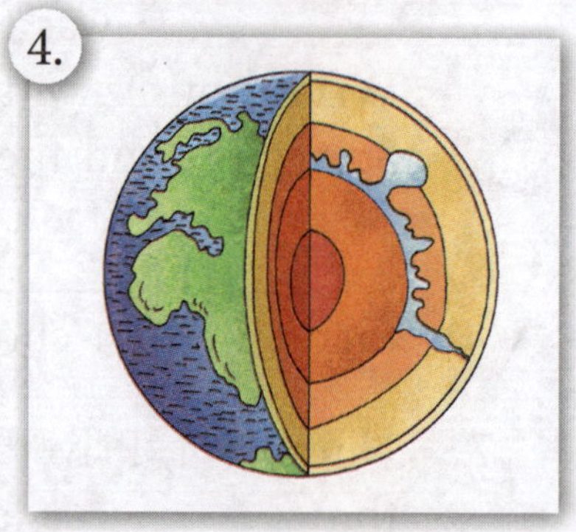

5.

6.

7.

a. Hydel

b. Thermal

c. Solar

d. Nuclear

e. Tidal

f. Geothermal

g. Wind

B. *Arrange the steps in the process of hydroelectric power distribution from the source to the destination in the order that they take place. Use the boxes below.*

The correct order would be

1.

dam and power station

2.

high tension power line

3.

low tension power line

4.

substation

5.

electric meter

6.

home

7.

area transformers

8.

domestic power supply lines

COOL FACT

Some materials like crystals, ceramics, proteins, etc. when pressed, can produce a form of electricity known as piezoelectricity. Did you know that quartz watches use piezoelectricity too?

Quiz Yourself 1

1. In the book, *Treasure Island*, on what ship did the young boy Jim Hawkins go to sea in an adventure in which he found a great treasure?
2. Which little girl went to meet the Wizard of Oz with her companions—the Tin Man, the Scarecrow and the Lion?
3. At which place, now in Pakistan, was the 4,500 year old bronze statue of the Dancing Girl found?
4. Who wrote the popular children's book *Charlie and the Chocolate Factory*?
5. At which place in Rajasthan did India conduct nuclear tests in 1974 and 1998?
6. By what name do we better know the mountain known to the Nepalese as 'Sagarmatha'?
7. What name is given to the indentations or dips on the surface of a golf ball?
8. What does the G stand for in GMT?
9. Which veterinary surgeon wrote several books under an assumed name, which was in actual fact the name of a famous football player?
10. Who invented the modern seat belt, also called the three point seat belt, which has saved the lives of millions of people involved in car crashes?
11. With respect to a particular river, complete this list of European countries—Bratislava, Belgrade, Vienna and ____________________?
12. An *Abhanga* is a form of devotional poem from which state in India?
13. Which bird makes the longest annual migratory journey as the seasons change?
14. The Italian inventor Antonio Meucci is today considered to be the inventor of which famous invention?
15. In 1852 which stamp became the first postage stamp to be issued in India?

Quiz Yourself 2

1. Which country hosted as well as won the first ever FIFA football World Cup in 1930?
2. Which was the first animated film to be nominated for the Best Picture Oscar Award?
3. Of which adventure sport is David Belle considered to be the founder?
4. Which Indian Union Territory uses French as one of its two official languages?
5. Who was the first Asian to be awarded a Nobel Prize?
6. Which bridge in Australia is affectionately called 'the Coathanger'?
7. Which country whose name begins with a 'U' is one of the seven that end with the letters 'stan'?
8. What is the name of the holy book of the followers of Zoroastrianism?
9. Which British rower is the only person to win an Olympic Gold in five different Olympic Games?
10. Which renowned sarod player is the father of Ayaan Ali Khan and Amaan Ali Khan, who are also well-known sarod players?
11. Which famous National Park was the first to be established in South Africa?
12. Which famous comic book series was written and illustrated by the French team of Goscinny and Uderzo?
13. Which Indian Nobel Prize winner is the founder of the Bachpan Bachao Andolan?
14. What connects Atyrau in Kazakhstan, Orenburg and Magnitogorsk in Russia, Suez in Egypt and Istanbul in Turkey?
15. Two Indian hockey players have each won four Olympic medals. One is Leslie Claudius, who is the other?

Keys

Page 9: 1. ISBN; 2. autobiography; 3. fable; 4. novel;5. index; 6. pseudonym; 7. chapters; 8. hardbound;9. publisher; 10. glossary; 11. preface ;Middle Column answer: Bibliophile

Page 10-11: A. 1. aerobridge; 2. apron; 3. runway;4. hangar; 5. ATC tower; 6. aviation terminal;7. aviation fuel depot; 8. fire station; 9. taxiway;10. tractor trolley B.

Page 12-13: Across 1. Arctic Tern; 4. Kiwi; 5. Flamingo; 6. Owl; 9. Pelican; 11. Turkey; 12. Bower Bird Down 2. Cuckoo; 3. Hummingbird; 7. Weaverbird; 8. Spoonbill; 10. Crane

Page 14-15: A. 1. Nur Jahan; 2. Rani Chennamma; 3. Sanghamitra; 4. Rani Laxmibai; 5. Jijabai; 6. Ahilyabai Holkar; 7. Razia Sultan B. Sanghamitra, Razia Sultan, Nur Jahan, Jijabai;Ahilyabai Holkar, Rani Chennamma, Rani Laxmibai

Page 16: A. 1. Braille; 2. Insects; 3. Dice; 4. Ayurveda;5. Sextuplets; 6. Hexadactyly B. 1. France; 2. abdomen; 3. Australia; 4. 6E; 5. RajyaSabha; 6. Harry Potter and the Half-Blood Prince

Page 17: 1. g; 2. e; 3. f; 4. i; 5. j; 6. a; 7. h; 8. b;9. c; 10. d

Page 18-19: 1. know; 2. bough; 3. dough; 4. slough; 5. through; 6. beard; 7. bird; 8. bed; 9. bead; 10. suite;11. straight; 12. debt; 13. both; 14. there; 15. fear;16. lose; 17. rose; 18. cork; 19. work; 20. card;21. front; 22. sword; 23. thwart; 24. cart

Page 20-21: 1. c, iv; 2. d, i; 3. a, iii; 4. f, ii; 5. b, vi;6. e, v; 7. i, xi; 8. k, xii; 9. l, vii; 10. h, ix; 11. j, x;12. g, viii

Page 22-23: A. 1. b, 2. g; 3. d; 4. a; 5. f; 6. c; 7. e; 8. h B. 1. speed post, 2. money order; 3. post office counter; 4. house rent collection; 5. inland letter; 6. philatelist; 7. first day cover; 8. passport form collection

Page 24-25: Across 4. zorbing; 5. BMX; 6. rockclimbing; 8. skiing; 9. surfing; 10. trekking Down 1. caving; 2. paragliding; 3. motocross; 5. bungee jumping; 7. rafting

Page 26-27: Across 2. shishya; 4. kacheri; 5. kriti; 8. qawwali; 9. gharana; 10. ghazal Down 1. shruti; 3. abhanga; 6. thumri; 7. naghma

Page 28: 1. c; 2. a; 3. b; 4. h; 5. d; 6. g; 7. e; 8. f;9. i; 10. j

Page 29: 1. Lalitpur, Patan, Bhaktapur; 2. yeti; 3. Gurkha, khukri; 4. Sagarmatha, Kanchenjunga, Sikkim; 5. Karnali; 6. earthquake

Page 30-31: 1. Tokyo 21: 00; 2. San Francisco 4: 00; 3. Washington 07: 00; 4. London 12:00; 5. Colombo 17:30; 6. Rome 13:00; 7. Sydney 22:00; 8. Dubai 16:00; 9. Islamabad17:00; 10. Moscow 15:00; 11. Cape Town 14:00; 12. Rio deJaneiro 10:00

Page 32-33: 1. Tanakh, Jews; 2. Quran, Prophet Mohammad (PBUH); 3. Bhagavad Gita, Arjuna;4. Christianity, Jesus Christ; 5. Sikhism, Guru GranthSahib; 6. Zend Avesta, Parsis; 7. Gautama Buddha,Tipitaka; 8. Jainism, Mahavira

Page 34-35: 1. heir (given); 2. elation; 3. road; 4. giant;5. male; 6. early; 7. bare; 8. rest; 9. cocoa; 10. ruin;11. is; 12. see; 12. sly; 13. ugly

Page 36: 1-d-iv; 2-c-ii; 3-a-i; 4-b-iii; 5-e-vii; 6-g-viii;7-f-v; 8-h-vi

Page 37: 1. True; 2. True; 3. False, c; 4. True;5. False, a; 6. False, d; 7. True; 8. False, b

Page 38: MH 1, 7, 9 ; RJ 2, 5, 11; GA 3, 8, 12;GJ 4, 6, 10

Page 39: 1. 10; 2. 5; 3. 4; 4. 15; 5. 42; 6. 18; 7. 3; 8. 32

Page 40-41:

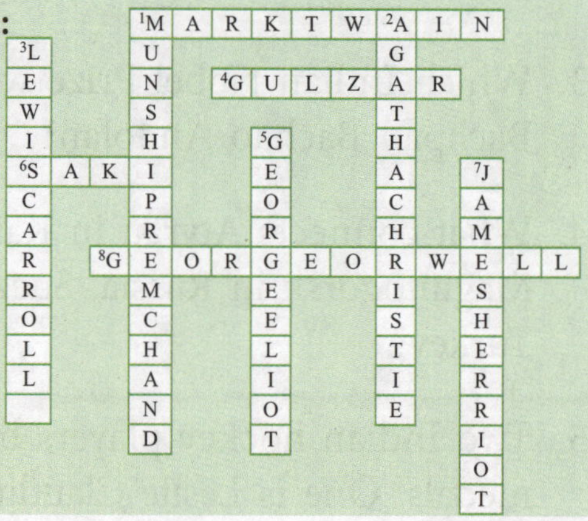

Page 44-45: A. Across 4. Rajiv Gandhi Khel Ratna; 8. Dhyanchand; 10. Bharat Ratna Down 1. Arjuna; 2. Bhatnagar; 3. Sahitya Akademi; 5. Dronacharya; 6. Dadasaheb Phalke; 7. Indira Gandhi; 9. Jnanpith B. 1. Bhimsen Joshi; 2. Ustad Bismillah Khan; 3. Satyajit Ray

Page 46-47: A. 1. c; 2. d; 3. a; 4. b; 5. f; 6. e B. 1. Bhopal Gas Tragedy; 2. Chernobyl Nuclear Disaster; 3. Deep water Horizon Oil Spill; 4. Fukushima Daiichi Nuclear Disaster; 5. The drying up of the Aral Sea; 6. Kuwait Oil Fires

Page 48: 1. f; 2. a; 3. d; 4. c; 5. e; 6. b

Page 49: 1. Brazil 2. Italy; 3. Germany; 4. Argentina; 5. Uruguay; 6. England; 7. France; 8. Spain

Page 50-51: 1. Toy Story; 2. The Lion King; 3. Home Alone; 4. How to Train your Dragon; 5. Finding Nemo; 6. The Sound of Music; 7. My Fair Lady; 8. Despicable Me; 9. Shrek; 10. Baby's Day Out; 11. Frozen

Page 52: 1. cars, cars; 2. guns; 3. hydrogen, oxygen;4. tricycle; 5. Benz; 6. motorcycle; 7. Ford; 8. Ambassador; 9. Padmini; 10. 800

Page 53: 1. b; 2. a; 3. a; 4. b; 5. a; 6. b; 7. c; 8. b;9. b; 10. a

Page 54: 1. Proxima Centauri; 2. constellation; 3. BigBang Theory; 4. black hole; 5. astronomy; 6. galaxy 7. Ursa Major; 8. Jupiter; 9. Light Year; 10. Halley's Comet; 11. Venus Acrostic aeronautics

Page 55: A. 1. Wimbledon; 2. Sama, Atharva; 3. kirpan, kanga, kachehra; 4. Humayun, Akbar, Jahangir, Shah Jahan; 5. Puducherry, Daman & Diu, Dadra & Nagar Haveli, Chandigarh, Lakshadweep; 6. hit wicket, handled the ball, hit the ball twice,obstructing the field, timed out B. 1. Tennis Grand Slam Tournaments; 2. The Vedas; 3. The 5 Ks of Sikhism; 4. Great Mughal Emperors; 5. Seven Union Territories; 6. Ten ways of getting out in cricket

Page 56-57: A. 1. i; 2. g; 3. f; 4. b; 5. h; 6. e; 7. j; 8. a; 9. c; 10. d B. 1. b; 2. e; 3. g; 4. a; 5. f; 6. j; 7. h; 8. i; 9. c; 10. d

Page 58: 1. Ranji; 2. Rani of Jhansi; 3. Santosh; 4. Beighton; 5. Jaipur; 6. Nehru

Page 59:

P	O	K	I	U	Y	T	R	E	W	Q	L	K
M	T	A	E	K	W	O	N	D	O	H	H	J
U	T	R	B	C	X	Z	A	S	D	F	G	J
A	Z	A	A	B	V	V	A	B	N	N	M	U
Y	I	T	U	O	Y	T	I	R	E	W	Q	J
T	K	E	N	D	O	H	K	U	N	G	F	U
H	K	H	T	U	N	K	I	Y	G	M	Z	T
A	W	E	R	J	T	Y	D	U	I	O	P	S
I	Q	W	E	R	T	V	O	N	M	R	T	U

Page 60-61: A. Whales 1. False; 2. True; 3. True; 4. False; 5. True; 6. True; Sharks 1. True; 2. True; 3. False; 4. False; 5. True; 6. True; B. 1. Baleen Whale; 2. Sperm Whale; 3. Humpback Whale; 4. Grey Whale; 5. Dwarf Shark; 6. Mako Shark; 7. Nurse Shark; 8. Hammerhead Shark; 9. Tiger Shark; 10. Thresher Shark; 11. The Great White Shark; 12. Basking Shark; 13. Angel Shark; 14. Wobbegong Shark; 15. Swell Shark

Word search grid

W	A	S	D	F	G	P	N	B	M	I	Y	V	W	T	H
O	T	H	R	E	S	H	E	R	S	H	A	R	K	Q	A
B	I	Z	Y	O	M	Q	S	P	D	L	H	J	B	B	M
B	G	R	E	Y	W	H	A	L	E	V	S	Y	P	A	M
E	E	R	T	W	Q	M	B	C	X	Z	Y	U	I	S	E
G	R	E	A	T	W	H	I	T	E	S	H	A	R	K	R
O	S	P	O	S	T	G	F	D	S	A	L	K	J	I	H
N	H	U	M	P	B	A	C	K	W	H	A	L	E	N	E
G	A	N	G	E	L	S	H	A	R	K	T	Y	U	G	A
S	R	N	U	R	S	E	S	H	A	R	K	B	P	S	D
H	K	P	O	M	U	Y	T	R	E	T	M	B	N	H	S
A	R	T	D	W	A	R	F	S	H	A	R	K	G	A	H
R	Y	U	I	H	N	B	V	R	O	P	A	S	D	R	A
K	F	G	M	A	K	O	S	H	A	R	K	H	I	K	R
S	W	E	L	L	S	H	A	R	K	S	G	L	K	J	K
V	B	A	L	E	E	N	W	H	A	L	E	X	B	N	R

Page 62-63: B. 1. China; 2. Sweden; 3. Italy; 4. Brazil; 5. Spain; 6. USA; 7. Switzerland

Page 64-65: 1. London Bridge; 2. tallest; 3. England; 4. San Francisco; 5. Coathanger; 6. Rialto

Page 66-67: ACROSS: 3. Cheraw (Mizoram); 6. Singhi Chham (Sikkim); 8. Thang La (Manipur) DOWN: 1. Bagurumba (Assam) 2. Bardochham (Arunachal Pradesh); 4. Hojagiri (Tripura); 5. Bihu (Assam); 7. Chang Lo (Nagaland)

Page 68-69: A. 1. 000-099; 2. 200-299; 3. 400-499;4. 100-199; 5. 700-799; 6. 900-999; 7. 000-099;8. 300-399; 9. 500-599; 10. 600-699; 11. 800-899;12. 600-699; 13. 000-099; 14. 800-899; 15. 900-999;16.

300-399; 17. 700-799; 18. 800-899; 19. 100-199;20. 800-899

Page 70-71: A. 1. Poland; 2. Switzerland; 3. Finland;4. Netherlands; 5. Ireland; 6. Swaziland; 7. Iceland;8. New Zealand B. Kazakhstan, Turkmenistan, Tajikistan; Uzbekistan;Kyrgyzstan; Pakistan, Afghanistan C. East Timor; South Africa; Central African Republic,South Sudan Cool Activity 1 a. Oman; b. Qatar; c. Yemen Cool Activity 2 a. Belgium, Netherlands, Luxembourg; b. Australia, New Zealand; c. Spain, Portugal;d. Norway, Sweden, Finland, Denmark, Iceland

Page 72-73: 1. US, Phelps, total, bronze; 2. Al, throw,consecutive, 1956; 3. Finnish, Flying, three, Olympic;4. 1936, person, gold, Games; 5. athlete, won, consecutive, 92; 6. Soviet, Latynina, record, 2008; 7. Munich, record, event, Mark; 8. Nadia, goldmedals, ten, Summer; 9. rower, Redgrave, only, five;10. hockey, silver, Claudius, Udham

Page 74-75: 1. c, i; 2. d, ii; 3. a, iii; 4. e, iv; 5. b, v; 6. h, vi; 7. i, vii; 8. j, viii; 9. g, ix; 10. f, x

Page 76-77: 1. tabla; 2. sitar; 3. flautist; 4. santoor; 5. sarod; 6. veena; 7. flute; 8. mridangam; 9. mandolin; 10. ghatam; 11. violinist; 12. shehnai

Page 78-79:

A	H	I	P	H	O	P	B	T	Y	B	E	L	L	F	A
C	O	E	J	L	S	C	P	K	O	Q	S	U	A	G	J
D	P	F	I	P	A	J	O	Z	C	B	S	A	M	B	A
S	A	L	S	A	D	N	L	M	H	D	F	H	B	F	Z
G	K	H	Q	H	P	R	K	C	A	G	I	K	A	H	Z
K	M	R	D	I	T	C	A	N	C	A	N	G	D	E	K
N	O	V	R	Y	J	L	O	S	H	B	I	F	A	J	L
U	S	X	A	V	M	F	T	W	A	Z	O	L	X	Y	M
T	A	N	G	O	N	O	U	D	C	P	R	A	N	W	Z
W	M	R	O	V	A	X	Q	S	H	T	U	M	D	A	G
Z	A	Q	N	V	X	T	A	R	A	N	T	E	L	L	A
A	N	Y	D	W	B	R	J	M	O	Q	U	N	Y	T	X
C	F	W	A	X	S	O	D	O	R	I	Z	C	A	Z	D
V	K	S	N	I	N	T	W	E	G	J	C	O	T	L	Q
B	R	L	C	F	I	K	M	O	R	U	W	A	I	D	V
H	P	B	E	L	L	Y	D	A	N	C	E	N	P	S	T

Page 80-81: 1. 11; 2. Cape Town; 3. Jackass Penguins;4. Apartheid; 5. Robben Island; 6. Table Mountain;7. Cape of Storms; 8. de Villiers; 9. 2010 FIFA World Cup; 10. Kruger; 11. Dutch; 12. Protea; 13. Authors/writers; 14. diamond

Page 82: 1. g, i, j; 2. a, d, h; 3. m, n, o; 4. c, e, f;5. b, k,l; 6. p, q, r

Page 83: 1. TV (image 4); 2. Telephone (image 5); 3. Refrigerator (image 6); 4. Air conditioner (image 3); 5. Vacuum cleaner (image 1); 6. Washing machine (image 2)

Page 84-85: A. 1. c; 2. e; 3. d; 4. a; 5. f; 6. g; 7. b E. Spelling of Mnemonic

Page 86-87: A. 1. d; 2. b; 3. j; 4. e; 5. g; 6. f; 7. c; 8. h;9. i; 10. a B. 1. Hearts; 2. Oliver Twist; 3. Malgudi; 4. treasure,island; 5. Dorothy; 6. Willy Wonka; 7. Dursley;8. Neverland; 9. Tributes; 10. Little Prince

Page 88-89: A. 1. a; 2. e; 3. b; 4. f; 5. c; 6. g; 7. d B. 1, 2, 4, 3, 7, 8, 5, 6

Page 90: 1. Hispaniola; 2. Dorothy ; 3. Mohenjo Daro; 4.Roald Dahl; 5. Pokharan; 6. Mt Everest; 7. Dimples; 8. Greenwich; 9. James Alfred Wight (James Herriot); 10. Nils Bohlin; 11. Budapest (all are 4 capital citiesthrough which the Danube flows); 12. Maharashtra; 13. Arctic Tern; 14. Telephone (Alexander GrahamBell is credited with the first practical workingtelephone); 15. 'Scinde Dawk';

Page 91: 1. Uruguay; 2. Beauty and the Beast; 3. Parkour; 4. Puducherry; 5. Rabindranath Tagore; 6. Sydney Harbour Bridge; 7. Uzbekistan; 8. Zend Avesta; 9. Steve Redgrave; 10. Amjad Ali Khan; 11. Kruger National Park; 12. Asterix; 13. Kailash Satyarthi; 14. Cities that are each spread over two continents; 15. Udham Singh